My Lunch with Marilyn ... and Other Stories

My Lunch with Marilyn ... and Other Stories

Stanley Price

Collated and edited by Munro Price

First published in Great Britain in 2023 by Sandycove

Copyright © the Estate of Stanley Price 2023

Edited, designed and produced by Tandem Publishing
http://tandempublishing.yolasite.com

The publisher is grateful to *The Oldie* Magazine for permission to publish these pieces.

Cover images, clockwise from top left: Marilyn Monroe, Benito Mussolini, Sophia Loren, Gloria Swanson, Noël Coward, Dennis Nilsen, Graham Greene, Mandy Rice-Davies, Maureen Lipman, Laurence Olivier, Stanley Price, Duchess of Argyll.

ISBN: 978-1-3999-6515-6

10 9 8 7 6 5 4 3 2 1

A CIP catalogue record for this book is available from the British Library.

Printed and bound in Great Britain by CPI Group (UK) Ltd, Croydon CR0 4YY.

Contents

Foreword

Stanley was Irish with no accent to prove it. Stanley was Jewish with no membership to prove it. Stanley was Waspish but rarely WASP.

Stanley was brave enough to be a show-business journalist in sixties New York but scared enough, in search of a cinema showing the Chinese film *In The Mood*, to scuttle, crab-like, across Leicester Square as though pursued by many wolves.

In the cast of the *Odd Couple* he would have been Felix, the fastidious one. Fluent in his French he would have identified with the silent and put-upon Monsieur Hulot.

He was a quietly unshowy and elegant writer who numbered Sir Antony and Sir Ronald among his friends. Neither 'Sir' nor 'Stan' would have suited him.

He was erudite, airy, emotional, dry, witty and intellectual but wore his gifts lightly and never on his sleeve.

He could pull a major prank on a genially gullible man like my late husband Jack Rosenthal. When they alongside Simon Gray transported a large and largely worse for wear lady writer back to her basement flat in Belsize Park, he followed up by writing a thank-you letter, purporting to be from her to Jack. It accused him of losing her cats and stealing one of her scripts. Jack was blamelessly mortified. It was at least three weeks before Stanley let the cat, not to mention the script, out of the bag by means of the slightest twitch of one lip.

When he and I performed readings from his charming,

evocative memoir, *Somewhere to Hang my Hat*, at various festivals and bookshops, he proved to be, like so many seemingly shy authors, an expressive and droll actor. He never pulled me up on my dodgy Dublin accent, proving him to be a kind man, and certainly a diplomatic one.

His adaptations of Noël Coward and Romain Gary stories for television were a fine fusion of their mutual talents and his plays for stage were nuanced reflections of the satirical observations of life, and his own life in particular, as two kinds of outsider.

His splendid book *James Joyce and Italo Svevo: The Story of a Friendship* analyses the similarities and co-dependency of the two great modernists. It adds a new depth to the origins of Leopold Bloom and deepens understanding of another exiled Irishman and an assimilated Jew.

He was a fine friend and a modest man. A great listener and a hearty, laughing audience. I miss him in my neighbourly life and I really do look forward to reading his oeuvre, although oeuvre is not a word Stanley would have used, except perhaps ironically.

– Maureen Lipman

Introduction

Stanley as a Writer

… he seems to me one of the few postwar British novelists who has managed to break down the distinction in this country between 'highbrow' and 'popular' fiction: who writes … novels of considerable intelligence and intellectual range which are also extremely funny, with a wit not confined in subject or viewpoint to a single class. In this, he comes closer to a certain type of American novelist … Richard Condon, Peter de Vries, Richard Stern and Joseph Heller, and I'd say he is the only British humourist who matches them at their best.

This puts him somewhat ahead of average British taste – the audience he appeals to here is still a limited one, but people who respond to his work, I've found, do so with extravagant enthusiasm. This came out in the reviews of his play *Horizontal Hold*, last season, which divided the critics, but struck two or three of us as the funniest, most truthful comedy of contemporary English life for some years. I was glad to find that this opinion was not simply that of a friend and coeval, since it was shared by Noël Coward!

These words come from an appreciation of Stanley by the immensely erudite *Observer* theatre critic, Ronald Bryden, in October 1967. Although Ron was a great friend, it is the shrewdest and most acute assessment I've seen of Stanley's work. Stanley was a wonderful writer, who rarely put a word out of place, wrote with great economy and elegance, and was extremely, sometimes hilariously, funny. He applied these qualities across a remarkable range of writing – journalism, novels, stage and TV plays and films – in a career of sixty-two years. Yet for all his talents he remained, in my admittedly partial view, slightly underrated, and I think that Ron's appreciation pinpoints the reason why. Stanley always ploughed his own furrow, regardless of – and sometimes in opposition to – the fashions of his day. From the beginning he was a rebel, and he remained one to the end of his life.

Ironically, Stanley began as a writer by rebelling against a rebellion: kitchen-sink drama. His most successful novel, *Just for the Record*, published in 1961, was a satire on the movement which still makes one laugh out loud today. It is the story of George Plumb, the son of a chief cashier in Birmingham incinerated while firewatching in 1942, who goes to London, changes his name to James Breedin, invents a working-class background of extreme brutality in Tiger Bay, writes a novel about it, and becomes an overnight literary sensation. *Just for the Record* was enthusiastically reviewed, especially in the *Sunday Telegraph*: 'With one blissful bang this sends up room-at-the-top-style novelists, kitchen-sink playwrights and a host of related types – and how we have awaited the happy hour of that detonation.'

Clearly this did not make Stanley many friends among kitchen sink novelists and playwrights, nor of the critics who admired their work. On his side, however, Stanley was more nuanced. He disliked *Room at the Top* and was once verbally abused by John Osborne, but admired Alan

Sillitoe and got on well with Arnold Wesker, whom for some obscure reason he always referred to as 'the Blessed Arnold'.

Stanley's next two West End plays were significant successes. Both were 'serious comedies', using humour and sometimes farce to examine wider contemporary issues. *Moving*, produced in 1980, dealt with the traumas of moving house, inspired by several surveys showing that next to bereavement and divorce this was the most stressful experience of ordinary British life. *Why Me?*, produced in 1985 in the midst of the Thatcher era, centred on a middle-aged engineer who loses his job and on the personal upheavals that come in its wake. John Peter in *The Sunday Times* called it 'an important event in British theatre: the first-time unemployment has been made the subject of a West End comedy... It's something between a realistic farce and a situation tragedy – a sitrag, as opposed to a sitcom.'

In the 1990s Stanley moved from writing stage to television plays. *Close Relations*, shown in 1990, tackled perhaps the last remaining modern taboo: incest. Based on a much-publicised recent court case involving a long-separated brother and sister, it won the Reims International Television Festival's best screenplay award for that year. Next came *Genghis Cohn*, a wonderful comedy of the deepest black, based on a novel by Romain Gary. A reworking of the Jewish legend of the *dybbuk*, a possessing spirit, its hero is the *dybbuk* of a Warsaw Jewish nightclub comedian, Genghis Cohn. Murdered in the Holocaust, Genghis returns to revenge himself on the SS captain who killed him by entering his body and making him a Jew. It won the best film award, again at the Reims Festival, in 1995.

In his later years Stanley changed medium once more and wrote two remarkable books, both of which, in different ways, marked a return to his Jewish roots. *Somewhere to Hang my Hat*, published in 2003, was a poignant and beautifully written memoir of his early life, dominated by his background as an Irish Jew. *James Joyce and Italo Svevo: the Story of a Friendship*, which appeared in 2016, was a study of the friendship between one of his literary heroes, James Joyce, and the great Italian Jewish novelist Italo Svevo, which began during Joyce's years in Trieste. Jan Morris, herself the author of an evocative book about Trieste, described it as 'admirable ... so rich in detail and characterisation.' This was Stanley's last work.

As well as writing these books, and encouraged by his great friend Jeremy Lewis, from 2002 Stanley also became a regular contributor to *The Oldie*, and wrote thirty-three pieces for it over the next twelve years. They look back on the most memorable encounters of his life as a writer. They have a cast to die for: Marilyn Monroe, Noël Coward, Gloria Swanson, Laurence Olivier, Sophia Loren, Gregory Peck, Maureen Lipman, Woody Allen, the Duchess of Argyll, Benito Mussolini, and many more. They are also often side-splittingly funny, and contain some of his best writing. Here they are collected in one volume, a small tribute to a wonderful writer and an inimitable man.

– Munro Price

THAT'S LIFE

The 'brain drain' to the US started in the late 1950s. I didn't feel any part of it. That was for brilliant scientists and thrusting businessmen, not for recent arts graduates, but I did have the practical advantage of a generous American cousin willing to sponsor me.

Having failed to find a job on Fleet Street, I thought, with the crazed naïveté of youth, that it might be easier in New York. It wasn't, but after the downbeat doldrums of fifties Britain, America hit one with its amazing energy and I caught enough of it to persevere in my job hunt. After four hard months, I got a job as a trainee reporter on *Life* magazine.

Slowly and painfully, I learned the arcane skills of working for *Life*. I became the token Englishman. My prose was constantly fine-combed by the department editor for anglicisms and other infelicities. Why that mattered I could never understand, as the much-edited prose of the reporters never reached the great American reading public. On *Life* the reporters saw all the action, going out on stories with photographers. Back in the office we wrote everything up at great length, and this went into a research file. If

1

the managing editor decided to run a particular story, a layout was done containing the best pictures, maybe a half-dozen from 300. Blocks of text were measured out, and the relevant editor pulled out the research and stayed in the office till early morning, trying to fit the gallons of information into the pint pots of text.

Life was highly labour-intensive. In New York there were upwards of sixty reporters working for fifty or so editors, not to mention thirty or so staff photographers. In addition there was a vast network of domestic and international bureaux. I don't believe any Press baron has ever rivalled Henry Luce in the size or quality of his empire. *Time* and *Life* were the world's leading weekly news magazines, and *Sports Illustrated* and *Fortune* were the leaders for sport and big business.

I managed to work my way through the domestic news desk, education, special projects and finally into the jealously guarded nirvana of the entertainment department. Both on and off-Broadway were having exceptional seasons, and I had my first serious sight of Eugene O'Neill, Tennessee Williams and Arthur Miller, and discovered the first productions of Edward Albee and Neil Simon.

The Hollywood studios were having a final flourish before independent production cut deeply into their monopoly of power. I became thoroughly spoilt, seeing new films in the silent luxury of screening-rooms and having expense-account lunches with their stars and directors who knew that a story in *Life* was worth thousands of dollars of free publicity for their movie.

One lunch, however, was memorable. About once a

month Henry Luce held a luncheon for himself and senior *Life* editors to meet a distinguished guest who was currently in the news. The relevant department was responsible for the invitation and for sending their junior reporter to collect and escort the guest to the penthouse dining room in the Time-Life Building. As a reward the reporter had lunch at the bottom of the table. The month I arrived in the entertainment department Henry Luce's guest was Marilyn Monroe, and I went in the hired limousine to collect her at the Waldorf Astoria.

Marilyn had just made *Some Like It Hot* and her much-publicised marriage to Arthur Miller was having an equally well-publicised break-up. There was a ten-minute wait before she came across the foyer. She wore a long camel-hair coat with its high collar turned up, a scarf round her hair and large sunglasses. It was clearly Marilyn Monroe – incognito. She raised her glasses and smiled when she said 'hello'. It was a lovely smile that disappeared as the glasses came down again. On the way out to the car a woman recognised her and asked for her autograph. Marilyn, glasses still down, quickly signed her name on a bit of paper. The woman looked at me, paper still at the ready. I could see the indecision on her face. 'It's OK,' I said. 'I'm not anybody.' Marilyn and I got into the back of the car.

Soon after having this experience I gave up telling people that I'd had it. My listeners invariably asked, 'What was she like?' The only answer I could give was 'Very nervous.' It was not what my questioners wanted to hear, but sadly people who are very nervous are not gorgeous, sexy or alluring.

She wanted to know what Henry Luce was like. Who else would be there? What would be required of her? I had only seen the world's then most powerful publisher once and he had struck me as a grim-faced old curmudgeon. I assured Marilyn he was charming and sympathetic, as were all the senior editors. They were probably more nervous about meeting her than she was about meeting them.

'You're English, aren't you?' she said. I admitted it. 'I worked with Laurence Olivier last year. He's wonderful,' she said. My sharing a nationality with Olivier seemed briefly to comfort her. But going up in the lift at the Time-Life Building she reverted to very nervous again. 'I don't know why I agreed to have this crazy lunch,' she said.

When we got out she asked where the 'powder room' was. I directed her. 'Don't go away. Please wait,' she said. I waited. I looked at my watch. We were already 20 minutes late for lunch. I thought I ought to go and make some explanation. I opened the door of the executive dining room and went in. Twelve pairs of eyes, including Henry Luce's, turned towards me. It is impossible to describe the expression on the faces of men who are expecting to see Marilyn Monroe in the flesh and instead see me. 'What's the matter?' Henry Luce said. 'Did you lose her?' It was the only remark he ever addressed to me.

'No. She … er … is in the Ladies. I think … er … she's … er … a little nervous.'

Fortunately, one of the company was a woman, the entertainment editor Mary Leatherbee, a wondrously tough woman who had piloted transport planes during the war. 'I'll deal with it,' she said. She pushed me into my place and went out. After a tense five minutes she returned with our guest. Either Marilyn had taken something in the toilet or she had been hypnotised by Mary Leatherbee. She appeared much calmer, and without her coat, scarf and dark glasses looked almost like her publicity photos, though agreeably more human. She went and sat next to Henry Luce. Halfway through lunch I glanced up the table. Marilyn was smiling and laughing and she had them all, even Henry Luce, in the palm of her hand.

After lunch it was Mary Leatherbee who took her back to her hotel, but as she passed me at the bottom of the table Marilyn said, 'Thanks for looking after me.'

Three years later she was dead. I heard the news at dinner in someone's house back in London. I thought it best not to mention how I'd taken her to lunch and what a terrific time we'd had together.

My Moll Mandy

'I think he needs to go walkies.'

Mandy's smile was irresistible, especially when it went with a low-cut eighteenth-century dress. Her dog was a big, fluffy, white chow. On its lead, I took it out of Monty Berman's theatrical costumier down Panton Street and into the Haymarket. I wasn't anxious to meet anyone I knew and have to explain myself. The dog, with stylish timing, waited till we reached the august pillars of the Theatre Royal before it cocked its leg.

'That's not your dog, is it?' Nick wasn't a reporter on the *Sunday Times* for nothing. I'd known him since college and he knew I wasn't a fluffy white chow man.

'No. I'm walking it for somebody.'

'Whose is it?'

I couldn't resist saying, 'Mandy Rice-Davies's.'

Only six months before, Mandy had appeared in the dock of the Old Bailey in the Stephen Ward trial. The aftermath of the Profumo affair was still sinking in with a shocked but titillated public.

'Do you want to tell me any more?' he said.

'Not really,' I said.

'Must dash then. Got to feed Christine Keeler's cat.' Nick was always good on exit lines. I walked the relieved dog back to his mistress.

Before explaining my relationship with Mandy I should explain my relationship with Michael Heseltine and Clive Labovitch. In 1960 they had, as ambitious young magazine publishers, bought a fading men's fashion magazine called *Man About Town*. They aimed to transform it into a trendy, glossy, quasi-literary magazine, a British *Esquire*. They abbreviated the title to *About Town*. Some issues later it was further abbreviated to *Town*. The joke on Fleet Street was that the frequently cash-strapped magazine would next be called *Own*, then *WN*, finally *N*, before disappearing. In fact it stayed as *Town* till its demise in 1967. The magazine was at its most successful in 1963-64, a period when I was, not coincidentally, its features editor.

After the *Lady Chatterley* case there had been a great tide of mildly (by today's standards) pornographic books. One of these was *Fanny Hill*, a classic eighteenth-century progress from haystack to boudoir. I spotted in a newspaper column that 'a well-known film producer', which in those days usually meant celebrated fly-by-night, was about to turn the book into a film, with Mandy Rice-Davies as the eponymous heroine. It had the smell of a great non-happening.

The entire editorial staff of *Town*, which consisted of the editor, Ronald Bryden, and myself, agreed that the chance to bring two famous courtesans together over the centuries was too good to miss. We would create some stills for a film that was probably never going to be made. Through her agent and for a fee, Mandy agreed to cooperate. Terry Donovan, one of the best and trendiest photographers of that epoch, was commissioned. I was sent off to explain the plot to Mandy and escort her to Monty Berman's for her fittings. It was a job for a junior reporter, if we'd had one, but I wasn't totally averse to meeting Britain's second most famous woman. In fact, she may even have been equal first with her friend Christine Keeler.

I picked her up at her flat, somewhere on what used to be called 'the wrong side of the Park'. Without make-up and in casual slacks and jumper, Mandy didn't look remotely like an infamous wicked woman, more a pretty sixth-former at a country grammar school. She was still only nineteen and her most lurid days were already behind her – friend of Keeler and Ward, sequentially mistress of Rachman, Savundra, Lord Astor et al. At first meeting, she was friendly, direct and funny. When I got to know her slightly better I realised that for her age and background she had tremendous confidence and a quality that had and would stand in her in good stead – chutzpah.

We went to Monty Berman's and, en route, discussed eighteenth-century literature. She was quick to see the parallels between her own and the Fanny Hill story, the young girl up from the country seduced by London high life. She put on some make-up, looked wonderful in the costumes and I walked her chow.

Terence Donovan was a burly, no-nonsense Cockney, one of a breed of talented photographers, several from the East End, who had cut their teeth in the fashion world. But he didn't come cheap, nor did Mandy. That was where our proprietors' money had gone. I was left to find very cheap extras to play the parts of sundry lovers and clients who would be in the photographs. I found a couple of actor friends willing to work for expenses and amused to share a four-poster with Mandy.

Labovitch and Heseltine turned up at the studio, ostensibly to keep an eye on their investment. They declined, even for economy's sake, to take part. Instead I was kitted out with a costume to pose as an elderly hair fetishist. Mandy entered cheerfully into the period spirit.

I was soon aware, from background whisperings, that something was bothering our proprietors. They seemed rather embarrassed to tell me what it was. After all, they both had good degrees from Oxford and what was worrying them was that Mandy wasn't showing quite enough... Labovitch gestured at his chest. I passed this on to Terry Donovan. I felt he would handle this better than me. He turned to Mandy, now posed on a chaise-longue: 'Mandy, love, bit more of the knockers.'

Mandy smilingly obliged. Terry Donovan took some great pictures. Everyone was happy. That issue with Mandy on the cover, leaning out of a stagecoach window en route to sinful old London, sold a record number of copies.

Mandy disappeared out of the headlines to crop up occasionally in the gossip columns. She modelled, did cabaret and got engaged to the odd foreign aristocrat. Fourteen years later a play of mine was produced in Israel and I took the opportunity to see the country with my wife and son. I also met Mandy again. She had been living there for the previous twelve years, having survived two wars and two husbands and become a patriotic Israeli without ever converting to Judaism. She also owned the most trendy restaurant and nightclub in Tel Aviv, and the director of my play had recently directed her in a Ray Cooney farce in Hebrew. He arranged for us to meet her at her restaurant and have dinner.

Mandy had weathered spectacularly well. Her memory was in good shape too. Almost immediately she remembered *Fanny Hill* and my performance as the elderly hair fetishist. After dinner she was deep in conversation with our son, aged fifteen, an avid historian. I eavesdropped tactfully. They were deep into Napoleon. Later our son told us how knowledgeable she was, especially about Catherine the Great's private life.

Mandy wanted to talk about the theatre. She was contemplating coming back to Britain as someone had offered her the lead in a play. She wondered if it was the sort of play that might go into the West End. Would I do her a favour and read it? I read it on the plane home. It definitely wouldn't make Shaftesbury Avenue, even allowing for Mandy's curiosity value. I wrote and told her so. She thanked me, but a year later I saw she hadn't taken my advice. She opened out of town and stayed out of town.

She did, however, settle quietly back in England. I never saw her again, but someone who occasionally hears from her told me that she has just drawn her DSS pension and spends half the year in Florida with her third, or possibly fourth husband. They have been married for twelve years. Clearly she has finally found Mr Right, though she calls him Mr Rubbish as he has made a fortune in waste disposal.

Recently I looked Mandy up on the Internet. There is no information about her or her current whereabouts, only endless repetitions of people quoting her most famous line. She said it to the prosecuting counsel in the Stephen Ward trial when he said that Lord 'Bill' Astor denied sleeping with her. 'Well, he would say that, wouldn't he?' I like to remember her that way – an unfazed eighteen-year-old standing up to the Establishment, showing the chutzpah that was her trademark and survival kit.

An Actor's Life for Me?

The year I first became interested in the theatre was 1947. Unfortunately that was also the year my parents packed me off to the sixth form of a boarding school in Cambridge to stop me being infected by disreputable company as well as a Cockney accent. But in the holidays I went to the theatre as often as I could, and at the Old Vic, for a one-and-ninepenny balcony seat, saw Olivier, Gielgud, Richardson and Guinness, not to mention Sybil Thorndike and Peggy Ashcroft. Inspired by them and ignoring the thousands of other equally inspired young people, I decided that I would be an actor. Naturally, I didn't tell my parents – they were already nervous enough about my falling into bad company. I must, however, have mentioned it to my local friends, as they insisted, when I was home for half-term, on taking me to their annual school production. There was a very good actor in it I ought to see, they told me. Besotted with the Old Vic, I went to the Hackney Downs grammar school's production of *Macbeth* in modern dress with a sinking heart. Fifteen minutes in, with Macbeth welcoming poor Duncan to his battlements, I had forgotten about the

Old Vic. My friends had been right about their school – it had a very good actor.

In his Scottish infantry officer's uniform, this Macbeth looked and sounded a lot more than his seventeen years. He moved with assurance and authority and was word-perfect. Most surprisingly for an untrained actor, his voice had range and resonance, and his accent had no trace of Hackney. I looked down at my programme to make a note of his name, worth remembering. Maybe one day I would see him again at the Old Vic. That name was Harold Pinter. I didn't see it on a programme again until thirteen years later, in 1960, when I went to see *The Caretaker* at the Duchess Theatre.

Afterwards, with my friends, I was loud in my praise of their *Macbeth*, but inwardly I was shaken. My ambition had taken a knock. Maybe there were dozens of brilliant schoolboy Pinters out there, heading for drama school en route to the Old Vic. I had played a few small parts in school plays, but would I ever be able to memorise a major Shakespearean role, let alone have the voice for it? I would soon find out. The Perse Players, the drama club of the school I'd been sent to, had a highly regarded annual production that was widely reviewed and they were about to do *Hamlet*. I was ambitious to play Laertes and do some fencing, or even age up a little for Claudius, perhaps Polonius. Instead, after auditions, our director, the history master, cast me as the Player King. I consoled myself that at least I had one big scene and several bravura cod-classical speeches, but even before rehearsals started several of these speeches had been severely cut. Worse was to happen. If Harold Pinter's Macbeth was the first nail in the coffin of my theatrical ambitions, it was Peter Hall's Hamlet that really hammered down the lid. As well as being head boy, P R F Hall, as he appeared in the programme, had a multiplicity of talents, theatrical, musical and academic. By the end of rehearsals I was thoroughly discouraged. I knew none of us aspiring thesps were remotely in the same class as Hall. At one point, to make more impact, I had thought about doing a Cockney or even an Irish Player King. In the end I modelled my accent on Hall's, which still had the merest touch of East Anglia.

On the first night I was overawed by his performance as were all the reviewers: 'A remarkable Hamlet given by an eighteen-year-old boy' (*Drama* magazine). 'His performance was consistent, graceful and done with great feeling' (*Times Educational Supplement*). There was no mention of the Player King.

Perhaps I was unlucky to encounter Harold Pinter and Peter Hall so early in my theatrical career. On the other hand, maybe I was lucky to learn so quickly that an actor's life was not for me. In the end it wasn't for Pinter or Hall, either. At the time it didn't break my heart. I would have to become something else, perhaps a writer, maybe even write a play. Later, at university, I did make a few final appearances on stage, my last being in a college production of *As You Like It*. I played William, a rustic in love with Audrey. I took the small part so that I could do my fall, a skill I had learned at the university judo club. I also blacked out my two front teeth to be a more convincing rural idiot. In my big scene with Touchstone, my rival in love, I let him push me to the front of the platform stage and at the final shunt I went right over and fell six feet into the front of the stalls. To gratifying gasps I got up unhurt. In retrospect, that seemed to symbolise my brief acting career.

Coincidentally, I discovered a while later that, though I didn't know her at the time, the woman I was to marry had been in the audience. She admitted that she hadn't recognised me when we eventually met – maybe it was the teeth – but she said she remembered my performance, or at least the fall. I promptly fell for her.

From time to time I see that Peter Hall is directing a play by Harold Pinter. I don't suppose either of them is aware of how they influenced my life.

HAMMING IT UP

Between 1949 and 1959 Jacques Tati made three films of comic genius, *Jour de Fête*, *Monsieur Hulot's Holiday* and *Mon Oncle*. It took him another thirteen years to make the next two, which were not as successful, and that was that. Tati, as I learned to my cost, was a perfectionist.

Tati came to New York to publicise *Mon Oncle*, and *Life* decided he was worthy of a 'picture essay'. I was chosen as the reporter, presumably on the grounds that I spoke the best English with a French accent. The photographer was the unusually genial, for a *Life* photographer anyway, Yale Joel. In my mind Tati was forever Monsieur Hulot, thin, stooping, hesitantly bird-like in movement. In person he turned out very well-built, straight and un-avian. In advance Yale and I had decided that our story would be Tati's reactions to Manhattan. Given his visual genius it seemed impertinent to tell him what pictures we wanted. We would leave it to him. Tati liked the idea of going round New York responding to whatever took his fancy. We suggested it might be fun to photograph him in the raincoat, hat and umbrella of Monsieur Hulot. His face fell. 'But I have not brought them with me.'

I said ·
at me pi
taken hir
hat into ·
have the ·
search of ·

He was
slung Nev
Modem A
them all –
East Side.
pastrami sa
immense s:

piece of ham disengaged itself an
Joel was photographing happil
'It's no good,' Tati said. 'T
sandwich into my mou
ham so I can really
'Elastic?' we sai
'We put the
It won't sl
The
fly

tainous filli—g. The stringy pastrami was as hard to bite free from the sandwich as spaghetti, and in his exertions the coleslaw kept spilling up the rabbi's sleeve.

'That is it,' Tati said. 'Only in America are there such sandwiches. I do that for you. It makes funny pictures, yes?'

Next day the Hulot costume arrived. Tati put it on and was transformed. The short, bedraggled raincoat and battered hat made him taller and ganglier. He paced the hotel room for us like a short-sighted ostrich in search of a lost egg.

Meanwhile, for a considerable sum – money, in those palmy days, was never a problem for Time-Life – I arranged to borrow the lunch counter of a local delicatessen. Tati arrived and inspected the pastrami. It wasn't elastic enough for him, so he ordered the ham. It was a jumbo sandwich with mayonnaise and coleslaw. Tati took a bite. A long d hung down his chin.

e ham should stretch from the
. We need some elastic under the
ull it.'

elastic under the ham. Broad elastic or rubber.
ow in the picture.'

deli owner wanted us out by lunchtime. Time was
ng. Maybe a garage would sell me an inner tube I
could cut into strips. I rushed out onto Fifth Avenue. The
nearest garage was probably three miles away in the Bronx.
Opposite was the elegant Saks department store. I raced in
and asked the nearest salesgirl if she had any broad, thin
rubber. 'What for?' she asked.

'Just need it in a hurry.'

'How about elastic?' She produced a reel of thin elastic.

A brainwave struck. I got the elevator up to the lingerie
department. I found a salesgirl in a quiet corner.

'Could I see the cheapest corset you've got?'

Here, I could see her thinking, is a cheapskate with a fat
wife. 'What size foundation garment, sir?'

'It doesn't matter, but it must be pink.'

She produced a $20 pink foundation garment. I put
down a $20 note.

'Have you got any scissors?' I said. 'And don't ask me to
explain.'

She handed me a pair of scissors. She clearly had no
intention of asking a crazed pervert to explain anything.

I cut the elastic side panels from the foundation garment, took them and ran.

Back at the deli, time was running out. Joel said, 'Jeezuz, where have you been?'

'It's a long story,' I said, handing Tati the hard-won elastic panel. He reassembled the sandwich with the ham laid on top of the panel. He bit and pulled and Joel clicked away.

'It's no good,' Tati said.

'It's fine,' Joel said.

'No,' said Tati. 'The elastic is not stretchy enough. I have idea. We need surgical gloves. We cut the fingers off.'

I was out of the door, sprinting for the corner drugstore. I bought a pair of pink surgical rubber gloves, raced back and handed them to Tati. He couldn't cut the fingers off with a knife. The deli owner, by now convinced a story would appear in *Life* sending up his sandwiches, reluctantly brought Tati some scissors. He watched him remove the pink fingers, slit the glove and remake the sandwich again. Tati bit, Joel clicked, the stretch was wonderful, but the ham fell off.

'Still no good,' Tati said.

'Time's up,' the deli owner said.

'I know how to fix it,' Tati said. 'We do it perfect tomorrow.'

Out of Tati's earshot, Joel said, 'We don't do it perfect tomorrow. Somehow it ain't that funny any more.'

'I know,' I said, and for the first time I cursed a rabbi.

That evening I went over to Tati's hotel to talk to him about the art of comedy. I went up to his suite. He was sitting in a chair with a large ham sandwich in front of him, busy with a needle and thread sewing a piece of ham onto the doctored surgical glove.

Next day we went all over town taking pictures. Somehow the delicatessen and the ham sandwich got forgotten, but I couldn't help wondering what the chambermaid was telling the others: 'You'll never guess what I found in that crazy Frenchman's room!'

THE TROUBLE WITH STANLEY

In the sixties and early seventies American money kept the British film industry afloat. Directors, actors, and technicians all benefited – even British writers did. For a novelist or playwright to be summoned to write, or rewrite, a movie was historically akin to a struggling Renaissance painter or sculptor getting the call from a Doge or a Pope to do a ducal fresco or a papal ceiling. Film producers thus became latter-day Medicis. A writer, his hard-earned movie money nestling in his bank, could return to his novel or play in comparative comfort.

My Medici was Stanley Donen, a man whose work I admired enormously. He had directed most of my favourite Hollywood musicals, *On the Town*, *Singing in the Rain*, *Seven Brides for Seven Brothers*, to name but three. He was now working in London and employed me under a major misapprehension. He had optioned the rights to a thriller and had taken on Julian Mitchell to write the screenplay, except that Julian had never written one before. The answer was obviously to get someone more experienced to join him. Julian volunteered my name. We had only met a couple of times and I knew him mainly as a rival 'promising young novelist'. When, via my agent, I heard the suggested pay I was instantly and intensely grateful to him. Slightly less grateful when I discovered that, in a throwback to the old Hollywood studio system, we had to share an office and were expected to be there every day. Our office was in Stanley Donen's suite in the shadow of the Hilton on Park Lane.

It was nearly a week before Donen discovered that I too had never written a film before. Julian had been mis-informed, I never knew how, and blessedly passed on his misinformation. By then it was too late. Donen had already welcomed me, in his slight Southern drawl, with the imper-ishable line: 'My name is Stanley and your name is Stanley, but you're working for me, so from now on you're Charles.' And indeed for the rest of my employment I was called Charles. Stanley was a hard taskmaster.

We worked regular office hours and every forty-eight hours or so we presented what we had written and had tortuous and tormenting script conferences.

As simple, naïve novelists, we had sought strong, credible storylines, but this was the heyday of the James Bond film and plausibility was not wanted on this voyage. We struggled to keep track of the twists and turns that Stanley wanted us to incorporate. And, as a great admirer of Hitch-cock, he insisted that we dream up 'a cropduster'. This was the generic term born from the climactic scene in *North by Northwest* when Cary Grant is machine-gunned by a crop-duster plane in a field where no crops grow. We racked our brains but no 'cropduster' cropped up. Then Stanley came in one morning very cheerful. Coming to work, he had seen the answer – a big mobile crane with a ball-and-chain demolisher.

'Say Greg is standing in this bus queue in Park Lane. One of these cranes comes along. Cut to one of the baddies at the controls. We see the ball swinging towards Greg. He dodges just in time.'

Julian and I spoke with one voice: 'And the ball continues on its pendulum movement and demolishes the façade of the Hilton. An expensive movie this.'

We were not popular that day, and it was back to more sleepless nights. Eventually the scene was shot in the confined space of a building site with Greg, who was Gregory Peck and already signed up, and the heroine, Sophia Loren, running from the Arab villains. It was indeed to be a starry vehicle, though when Julian and I finally saw *Arabesque* we never did quite understand the plot.

In those three months we slaved in the galleys of the movie industry Julian and I earned enough money to go back to finishing our promising new novels in comfort. But, as I learned with Stanley, there is money and Money. One morning I went in to hear his secretary ordering him a new Mercedes Sports. I knew he had only recently bought himself an expensive new car. She explained this was for his wife's birthday. A few weeks later I heard the secretary enquiring about an aeroplane. Fascinated, I asked Stanley why he now wanted an aeroplane.

'We're just renting one,' he said. 'What for?' 'We're looking for a house in the country.' I clearly displayed incomprehension. 'In your country,' he said patiently, 'all the good houses are behind hedges up those long drives.

You can't see them from the road. You can only see them from the air.'

'But if you see something you like, how do you know it's for sale?' He smiled at the idiot he was employing: 'If you've got money, Charles, anything is for sale.'

I learned an enormous amount about money, film-making, even life, in my time with Stanley Donen. I saw him on telly last year being honoured at the Oscars and he is, bless him, still looking tanned and healthy. I suppose I feel good about him because I finally got even. On my last day in his employ we exchanged parting gifts. I gave him my latest novel. He asked me to inscribe it. I wrote: 'With best wishes to Charles Donen from Stanley Price.'

CONGRESS INTERRUPTUS

Before sex education, before Kinsey, Comfort and the many loves that finally dared to speak their names, most of us somehow managed to find out what constituted the best part of a private life. Our education usually came by word of mouth, mainly from our peers. There were also books that got passed around. In my time the most popular were Dr Eustace Chesser's *Love Without Fear* and any of the works of Dr Norman Haire that you could lay your hands on. I remember being astounded by some of the things included in his *Encyclopaedia of Sexual Practice*, even though I never got beyond 'H' before it was snatched away from me. I was particularly astonished that on the title page his credit was 'by Dr Norman Haire, President of the Sex Congress of Geneva'. My mind boggled at what went on at a Sex Congress, let alone in Geneva.

By the time I was called up for National Service, I reckoned I was sufficiently knowledgeable in sexual matters. The problem was finding the opportunity to apply one's knowledge. Despite all the foul language, filthy limericks and vile songs of my fellow National Servicemen I reckon there was a more than 50 per cent virginity rate. However, halfway through National Service, I had an unforgettable sexual experience. My oldest friend Wally and I were on leave in London at the same time. It was a Thursday night and we were looking for some affordable entertainment. I had bought a *New Statesman*, and going down the events columns a name leapt out at me – Dr Norman Haire. That evening at the Conway Hall, Red Lion Square, Holborn, he was addressing the Rationalist Society of Great Britain on 'The Rationalist Approach to Sex'. No question where we were going.

Since the 1930s the Conway Hall had been the meeting-place for a wide range of radical groups, from pacifist socialists through vegans and naturists to theosophists and the followers of Gurdjieff and Blavatsky. The audience that night looked like a cross-section of all of them. I suspected that some of the women in flowing smocks and dirndl skirts were naturists on a night out. A lot of the men were wearing tweed suits that looked homemade, worn with boots or sandals. Most surprisingly dressed of all when he appeared was Dr Norman Haire himself. He was wearing a baggy, bright purple corduroy suit. He was in his fifties, fat and had a large walrus moustache. Not exactly a figure one would associate with sex, rational or otherwise.

After a fulsome introduction by the chairman, Dr Haire was on his feet. His voice was loud and rather harsh. It is now half-a-century ago, but his opening lines are engraved indelibly on my memory. 'I am sorry but tonight I am going to shock you. So let's start with the worst first – necrophilia, sleeping with a dead body.'

There was such a massive intake of communal breath that it was as though all the oxygen had been sucked out of the room. I glanced at Wally. His jaw had dropped. 'You sleep with a dead body. You're put on trial. If you're found guilty you're given a ten- or twelve-year sentence. But who have you hurt? Nobody. Rape a young woman, bring an unwanted life into the world and what happens? The victim is humiliated in court and argued over. And, if found guilty, what does the man get? Three, maybe four years in jail. Is that rational? No. Nothing about our sex laws is rational.'

He launched into a free-ranging tirade against any kind of sexual repression. His technique was to proceed by a series of shocking and angry questions. 'Masturbation!' he shouted. 'Why is it called self-abuse? Why "abuse"? Nobody goes blind. Take it from me, it doesn't stunt growth. Why the word "abuse", then? To create guilt, that's why! Like everything else in our society concerned with sex.'

I sneaked a look round. Wally had managed to get his jaws back together, but his eyes looked very poppy. The rest of the audience remained frozen, aghast, clearly dreading the next awful perversion the President of the Sex Congress of Geneva would hurl at them. Of course, today nothing much he said would have unduly disturbed an average post-watershed TV viewer. But that evening in the Conway Hall, even for the most free-loving, vegetarian Trot, Dr Norman Haire was light-years ahead of his time. For a full fifty minutes he spared his audience nothing. No chink or kink of sexual behaviour escaped his attention. As he

built to a climax on consenting sadomasochism, sweating
profusely, walrus moustache glistening, arms outstretched,
he became for a moment a religious figure – a Messiah in
purple corduroy.

He sat down to a stunned silence. Then British politeness
overcame shock and there was some awkward applause.
The chairman asked for questions. After a long embarrassing pause a few hands went up in the air. Several halting,
innocuous questions were asked. The audience began to
unfreeze. As people whispered to their neighbours there was
a sort of background twittering. Hands were shooting up
on all sides. In the row in front of us a small, middle-aged
man had been waving his arm, trying desperately to attract
the chairman's eye. Finally the chairman acknowledged
him. The man got up nervously. 'Dr Haire, you mentioned
several forms of birth control. There was one I think you
didn't mention. Would you like to say something about …
er … other forms?'

'What other forms?' Dr Haire's tone was aggressive. 'What
is it?' The man mopped his brow with a handkerchief, voice
just audible. 'I'd rather not say – not in mixed company.'

Dr Haire was incredulous. 'Not in mixed company –
when we've already talked about necrophilia, coprophilia,
incest, sodomy, bestiality? Come on, what is it?' The man
mopped more and looked close to a heart attack. 'I'd rather
not say.'

Dr Haire leaned towards the man. 'What is it, then?
Condom – French letter? Dutch cap?' The man shook
his head. 'Douche? Ordinary pessary? Foaming pessary?'

The man kept shaking his head and mopping his brow. Dr Haire lowered his voice and spoke very slowly. 'Is it coitus interruptus – withdrawal?'

'Yes,' the man gasped. Dr Haire flew into an extraordinary rage. He pointed at the man, addressing the whole audience. 'For years this man has pestered me with letters and telegrams advocating this vile, disgusting method of birth control that demeans the very nature of the sexual act. It is foul and repugnant and not even very effective. Get him out of here. I will not talk while that man is in the hall.'

In a total silence Dr Haire sat down and folded his arms. His questioner, looking as though he was having the heart attack, sat down. Then two large, younger men appeared beside him and whispered something to him. Did the Rationalist Society of Great Britain have bouncers? The man was escorted from the hall. It was too much for Wally and me. We were both writhing with suppressed laughter. My ribs ached. My eyes were watering. We nodded at each other, got up and just made it out of the hall. Sitting on a bench there, his head in his hands, was the coitus interruptus advocate. Out in the street we doubled up, howling with post-traumatic laughter.

We were still laughing uncontrollably when we went into a pub a hundred yards up the street. It was hard to get our order out to the barman. 'Seen a funny film, have you?' he said.

I took a firm grip of myself. 'No. It was better than a film – much better.'

'How about sharing the joke, then?'

'Ever heard of Dr Norman Haire?' Wally said. The barman shook his head. 'Next time you see he's talking somewhere you've got to catch him.'

'What's he talk about?'

We couldn't tell him. The hysterics had returned.

LOST IN TRANSLATION

I had been spoilt. After a short tour, my first play had come straight into the West End. When my second one didn't I was hugely disappointed. It was like knowing all your friends were at a terrific party but you hadn't been invited. When the play finished its successful tour no London theatre was available. The tour was extended. It was one of those rare successful seasons and several other plays were in the same plight. We were like planes circling Heathrow waiting to land. Mine never came in, but went into theatrical mothballs. Inevitably, the stars dispersed into other lucrative employments and the playwright went home to lick his wounds, be comforted by his family and wonder what to do next – teaching, dentistry, MI5.

It was some consolation when my agent told me that a French producer, I will call him Marcel, had seen the play on tour and wanted to option it for a production in Paris. First, of course, it had to be translated. I was told the person Marcel had in mind was one of France's top play translators. Delighted though I was, I still enquired about my rights. I learned that I had the final approval over the translation. This would have been useless to me in any other language, but I felt my French was good enough to notice *si quelqu'un prenait des libertés avec mon oeuvre*. I signed the contract.

Life, creative and otherwise, went on and eventually I received the translation. On the whole I felt one of France's top play translators had done a fine job. Here and there I could have quibbled, but my agent had warned me about quibbling, particularly with a comedy. The translators had a trump card up their sleeve – you didn't appreciate their national sense of humour. What broke them up on Shaftesbury Avenue didn't necessarily roll them in the aisles on the Champs-Élysées. I limited my quibbles to the change of title.

The play was set in what used to be called a fat farm, before financial and linguistic inflation turned them into health clinics. It was intended as a satire on a society where people paid fortunes for a diet of lemon and water, grated carrot and maybe a yoghurt on feast days. I had rather liked my title – *The Starving Rich*. Marcel didn't like it. He said it sounded too much like Molière. *Un Yaourt Pour Deux* was the new title. I told Marcel I found the new title, 'how shall I put it – a little, er, broad'.

'*Mon ami*, you don't understand the French theatregoer. If they think they are going to see Molière and you don't give them Molière – *phut!*' Maybe I should have seen *l'écriture sur le mur* right then, but I didn't. Inevitably in the back of my mind was the thought that the British weren't doing my play and the French were. 'Paris', as a French king once said, 'was worth a Mass.'

Everything went quiet for a while and then I had a

jubilant call from Marcel. Francis Blanche was going to play the lead. Feeling wildly insular, I admitted I had never heard of Monsieur Blanche. Marcel was appalled. Blanche was perfect. He was fat. He was a huge draw. He was a great comedian, a really funny man. He had been married five times. His present wife was black. People said he had only married her so he could introduce her as 'Madame Blanche'. I was feeling increasingly uneasy. 'She's not going to be in the play too, is she?' I said. 'You are a funny man too,' Marcel said, a touch drily, I thought.

When the play went into rehearsal, Marcel phoned me. He had assembled a wonderful cast, some rewrites were being done, everything was impeccable. I spoke to my agent – I would like to see the rewrites, maybe help with them, go to a rehearsal or two. My agent reported back that Marcel said Monsieur Blanche was nervous with authors around. Blanche was *formidable*, everything was wonderful, I shouldn't worry. My agent said that Marcel was being very generous. He was not only paying for my wife and me to go over for the first night and stay in an expensive hotel, but paying for her and her husband too.

I spoke to a more experienced playwright. He said that unless you were an internationally famous playwright you never had much control over foreign productions. I still couldn't help feeling that my child was out there with alien foster parents and probably picking up some nasty foreign habits.

We had been warned that Parisian first nights were rather dressy, so when we arrived at our chic Paris hotel we changed into our London best. I had my first sinking feeling when

I looked at the posters outside the theatre. I was given the correct credit, but my top French translator was sharing his with Francis Blanche. When a star gets a writing credit you can smell a rat in any language.

Inside, the hospitable Marcel left us in the custody of his assistant, Yves, who sat with us in the sixth row. The curtain went up on a set that was recognisably a health clinic. After that things became increasingly unrecognisable, not just the dialogue but the action and the characters too. The inmates were all fat and comic, the staff nearly all female and provocatively dressed. Here trousers were dropped, girls stuffed into *armoires* and in the midst of it all was Francis Blanche, a Gallic version of the late Robert Morley, a Robert Morley on speed. Molière it wasn't.

Just discernible inside this fat French farce was the famished body of my original play. But the audience and Francis Blanche clearly loved each other, even when he digressed into a long, seemingly impromptu tirade on the corruption of the Paris police.

After two and a half hours it was over. The curtain came down to healthy applause. We headed for the exit. 'Where are you going?' our minder, Yves, asked. 'This is just the interval.' I noticed that Marcel was nowhere to be seen.

I don't remember much about the second half. I may have gone to sleep or had a nervous breakdown. When it was finally over I looked at my watch. In French my second play was marginally longer than *King Lear*. Marcel appeared to shepherd us backstage and into the star's dressing-room. I was introduced to the beautiful and very black Madame Blanche, and then her husband appeared, said,

'*Ah, l'auteur, le génie.*' He embraced me and I suddenly felt I was in the play. My trousers would fall down. I would be accused of sleeping with his wife. I would be shoved into a wardrobe. My French had deserted me. I may have mumbled '*Formidable*' to him, or maybe '*Je suis bouleversé*', which I was, but not just by his performance. I was in shock about the whole bloody thing.

Yves took us all, stunned and exhausted, to an expensive restaurant. Marcel was clearly keeping us separate from the main party just in case my French recovered enough to express an honest opinion. We drank a lot of good wine and at some point Marcel did appear and drape an arm round my shoulder. The advance booking was immense. The play was already a *grand succès*.

'I don't really deserve it,' I said. He was appalled. '*Pourquoi non, mon ami?*'

'You're not really doing my play.'

'*Mais oui, bien sûr.* The idea is yours. You deserve every credit.'

My agent was looking at me pleadingly. I knew what she was thinking. She was right. I didn't argue with Marcel. I did what all experienced writers have always done, in France as in as in England: *je pris l'argent et je courus.*

THREE MEN AND A CHAIR

I've only lunched at the Savoy Grill once. It was not an auspicious occasion, as a man at the next table had a heart attack and died while drinking his soup. Within seconds four waiters arrived, each took a chair leg, and the dead man was spirited away before anyone could be put off their lunch. This knowledge of how to deal with a dead weight was to come in useful some years later at a Dramatists' Club dinner.

Founded in 1909 by Pinero, Maugham and J. M. Barrie, the Dramatists meet for quarterly dinners at the Garrick Club as an opportunity to discuss, among other things, the devious ways of theatre managements and, more recently, of television companies. I frequently went to the dinner with a good friend and near neighbour, the recently departed and much-lamented Jack Rosenthal. I enjoyed driving him there because I usually got a fine earful of what a dog's dinner some director was making of his latest television play.

That particular evening there was a reasonable company, but I did notice that one guest was particularly the worse for wear. She had been, in her day, a successful playwright and screenwriter. I will call her Penelope. By the end of the evening she was with us in body only, a fairly substantial body too, as things turned out. Clearly someone had to get her home. We found her address in her handbag. She lived in Maida Vale, which unfortunately was on my way, and, of course, Jack's. I had also promised Simon Gray, another North Londoner, a lift. We three plus the comatose Penelope wouldn't all fit in my car. The porter at the Garrick summoned a taxi and we three plus the porter each took a chair leg. Jack went with her in the taxi. Simon and I followed in my car.

As ill luck would have it, Penelope lived in a garden flat down a spiral staircase. As she sprawled comatose in the back of the taxi, Jack extracted her keys from her handbag and I was deputed to fetch a chair. I let myself into the darkened flat, looked round and screamed. At least six pairs of eyes were glaring at me in the dark. I switched on a hall light. Six Siamese cats stared at me. I found an upright chair in the kitchen. Back in the street the taxi driver helped us get Penelope onto the chair and then he was off.

That left three of us and four chair legs. After some discussion Simon took the two front ones and Jack and I the back. We started the tortuous descent down the spiral staircase, Simon going down first. Inevitably the chair was at an angle and slowly and irrevocably Penelope slid forward and ended up on Simon's back. He staggered around with his considerable burden in the small front yard. We went to his rescue and half-carried, half-dragged her into her flat. The bedroom was at the end of the corridor. There was a double bed, a desk and the walls were lined with crammed

bookshelves. On the floor were piles of scripts, presumably
Penelope's entire oeuvre. We manhandled her onto the bed.
She appeared to come to slightly, her eyes flickered open,
her hands clasped tightly round Jack's neck. 'Don't go. I
love you, I love you,' she slurred.

Jack struggled unsuccessfully to release himself. Always
the gentleman, he didn't want to use excessive force. I
thought of his wife, the lovely Maureen Lipman, waiting
patiently at home for him in Muswell Hill. I bent down and
prised Penelope's hands apart. 'Goodnight,' we shouted,
making a run for it.

Back in the car Simon said, 'Did you see all those bloody
cats?'

'Did you see all those scripts?' Jack said. We should have
been laughing, but we weren't. Maybe we were thinking
that any writer could end up that way: a bedroom full of
scripts, a drink problem – and cats.

A few days later I wrote a letter to Jack. At the top of
the page I typed Penelope's address. I had played the odd
practical joke before, but I don't know what inspired this
one. Perhaps it was remembering Jack's remark about 'all
those scripts'. I wrote, as best I remember:

Dear Jack Rosenthal,
I am very grateful to you and your friends for seeing me
home safely on Friday night. I am, however, most upset to
discover that several of the scripts that were in my bedroom
are missing. I know you are a prolific television writer and
I must warn you that should I see anything of mine, or

anything based on my work, on television under anybody else's name, I would instruct my solicitors accordingly.

Then, remembering Simon's line about 'the bloody cats', I wrote:

PS: One of my cats is also missing.

I couldn't believe Jack would be fooled. The PS would surely tip him off. Next day Jack was on the phone reading me the letter, outraged. 'There's thanks for you. You break your back for some bloody stranger and that's what you get.'

To break a practical joke you have to own up fast and I missed the opportunity. Jack went on talking. 'And what does she think I want with her miserable cat? Maybe put the bloody thing into a telly play too. And why me? Why not you two?'

'You were the one she loved.'

'Terrific!'

And somehow that was it. There seemed to be no going back. Some time later I read somewhere that practical jokes are a sign of aggression. I thought about that carefully. Why would I want to be aggressive towards Jack? Was I envious that he was so prolific? That he stood up to directors? Surely neither. I came up with only one explanation. Despite all his closely observed television work Jack was, in many ways, an innocent. I sensed he was gullible and I, or a nasty little bit of me, wanted to test how gullible.

I can only plead that other people saw him that way too.

One was Willis Hall, another member of the Dramatists. He discovered we were having pheasant at one dinner and called the Garrick kitchens. He explained that his friend Jack was too diffident to call himself, but didn't like game and would prefer a Barnsley chop. On the night that is what a mystified Jack was served. But I know I shouldn't use someone else's behaviour to excuse my own.

A little while later, walking in Kenwood, I bumped into Jack and Maureen. Maureen said: 'Remember that mad woman writer? Thank God we never heard from her again.'

'No?' I said. I didn't get the intonation quite right. She was on to it like a flash.

'It was you!' she shouted. 'You!'

'You bastard!' said Jack. 'Bastard!'

Jack took it in such good part that I felt an even bigger rat. But we stayed good friends till his death in May. I don't do practical jokes any more.

I Once Met...

BOBBY FISCHER

It was my first assignment as a reporter on *Life* magazine and I was nervous. When the photographer, Doug Rodewald, arrived, he was puffing slightly under the weight of his equipment. He put it down between us like a challenge. I'd been told that a reporter should never help carry a photographer's equipment; it established the wrong relationship. But he was at least twenty years older than me and 40 pounds heavier. I picked up his tripod and a small box and told myself that I'd toughen up as I got more experienced. We drove off to Brooklyn to do a story on a twelve-year-old chess prodigy.

At the time Bobby Fischer was in the fourth grade of his local high school and regularly beating the best adult players in the country. He lived at home with his mother and I had to convince her that a story in *Life* could help her son's career without spoiling his character. Their apartment was on the first floor of a clapperboard house in a poor but still respectable part of Brooklyn. Bobby Fischer was tall and gangling, but with a physique that looked certain to fill out in a couple of years. Taciturn when I first met him, he was even more taciturn when introduced to Doug Rodewald. His mother, Mary, was around forty and worked

as a nurse. She was a tough-looking lady. Initially there had
been no mention of Bobby's father. I had to screw up a lot of
courage to get her into the kitchen and ask who and where
the father was. She didn't want him mentioned in the story.
Readers, I said, would at least want to know who he was.
If we didn't mention it at all it would attract even more
curiosity. Naturally we would mention it very discreetly.
She said quickly that she and Bobby's father had divorced
over ten years before. That was it. The subject was closed.
All this was said in a low whisper. His father was clearly not
a topic she ever discussed with – or in front of – Bobby, let
alone in front of a *Life* reporter and photographer.

The bleak, under-furnished apartment was obviously
not inspiring Doug Rodewald to flights of photographic
fancy. He tried engaging Bobby and failed. 'Great picture
story this is going to be,' he hissed at me. I knew that the
secret of photo-journalism in a static situation was that the
subject must become unaware of the camera. Either this was
achieved by the photographer clicking off so many pictures
that the subject forgot he was there, or by the subject being
distracted by the reporter's penetrating questions. Asking
Bobby Fischer questions proved a thankless task. He gave
monosyllabic answers and then glanced irritably at the
camera.

His mother was sensitive enough to realise my predica-
ment. She took me aside – 'Do you play chess?' I told her
I hadn't played for about four years and hadn't been very
good, even then.

'Try,' she said. 'It's the only way you'll get him to relax.'

There was no alternative. For the success of my first

assignment I would offer myself as sacrificial lamb to this disgruntled twelve-year-old.

'How about a game of chess?'

He looked at me with mild interest for the first time.

'You any good?'

'Bit rusty, but I wasn't too bad.' If I could hold him at bay for even half-a-dozen moves, Rodewald might get a few relaxed pictures.

'They're beautiful,' I said, as Bobby Fischer laid out a set of finely carved ivory pieces.

'I won them. You can be white.'

I remembered an opening I had used effectively at college. I made my moves very slowly. His moves came like lightning. For about four moves I felt I was holding my own and then I realised he was going to make a total monkey out of me. I was walking straight into one of the oldest traps in the game. Rodewald was taking his pictures infuriatingly slowly, and I was going to be demolished in minutes. I had to hang on at least for a few more moves.

Then, suddenly, a miracle – a glowing light shone round my queen's bishop, illuminating its path to king's knight 5; the way out of the trap. If only! I decided to sacrifice my knight, but he didn't take it. He had a smarter plan. A few moves later it was checkmate.

'You shouldn't have moved your knight,' was all he said.

'Beaten already?' Rodewald said, but he looked happy. He had his pictures.

Two days later we went to the prestigious Manhattan Chess Club and took pictures of Bobby Fischer beating a grandmaster. There were only about half-a-dozen of them in the US. The Club secretary assured me that one day, sooner rather than later, Bobby Fischer would be the first American World Champion.

Two years later Bobby Fischer became US chess champion. A year later he became an international grandmaster and qualified to challenge for the world championship. In 1972 in Reykjavik, at the age of twenty-six, he became world chess champion. Even before that he had been highly unpredictable and demanding. He soon became even stranger, and didn't play chess in public for another 20 years. In 1992, when Serbia was under American sanctions, Fischer defied his government and played Spassky in Belgrade. His passport was revoked and he was regarded as a traitor. He became wildly antisemitic and welcomed the 9/11 attack on New York. He was imprisoned in Japan while he awaited extradition to the US. Now he has been saved by Iceland. I hope he will be happy there and even start playing chess again. I doubt if I will. I haven't played since I lost to him.

WHAT'S THE CATCH?

If you've always wanted to write a novel, you feel pretty pleased with yourself when you've finally written one. If, even more wondrous, a publisher accepts it, a certain brief euphoria takes over. A literary future opens up like some exotic flower. The imagination can become feverish. Who could play the heroine in the television series? Or would it be better as a feature film? There is the speech to think about – the one that commiserates with the other fine novelists on the Booker shortlist whom you've just pipped to the post. I know because I've been there – except in my case the Booker Prize hadn't yet been invented and I happened to be living in America. That, however, made me eligible for a Pulitzer. Naturally, I would need a larger oeuvre to be considered for the Nobel, but I had plenty of time before worrying about that speech. In that brief period of euphoria, naïveté and hubris held hands. It is an embarrassing time to remember.

I had worked on my novel in the evenings and weekends. My day job was as a reporter on *Life* magazine and I had kept my moonlighting activity very much to myself. When I knew it was to be published I told a few friends. My stock went up at work, but there was one unwanted consequence.

I had a friend called Dick in the advertising department. He had a colleague called Joe whom he wanted me to meet. Joe had also just written a book but hadn't yet found a publisher. Anyway, Joe was a great guy, Dick said, and I would really enjoy him.

Dick arranged for the three of us to meet in a Sixth Avenue bar that had good Italian food. The plan was that he would have a drink and then leave us to have lunch together. I was starting to regret my decision already. It was shaping up to be like a really bad blind date. Joe turned out to be a big shambolic man in his mid-thirties with a heavy Brooklyn accent. At lunch it was a mistake for him to order spaghetti. When it arrived his relation to it was as a Hoover to fluff. It was not a pretty sight. At the same time I wasn't feeling too happy about my own attitude. With the insatiable curiosity of a true novelist, I should have been probing this man's life and times instead of being bothered by his clothes, accent and table-manners. Anyway, after a few self-deprecatory remarks about my own book, we talked about his. Everything he told me about it made my heart sink. It was yet another World War Two blockbuster – son of *From Here to Eternity*, I thought to myself. This thought allowed me to dismiss him, which was what I wanted to do. My lunch-companion, his spaghetti vanished, his plate hoovered clean, was spoiling my moment. I was the new novelist on the block and, for the time being, didn't want to know about any others. He told me his book was 900 pages long but his agent was persuading him to cut it to 500. I asked him the name of his agent. I'd never heard of her. I would probably never hear of him again either. I wished him luck and we parted without making another arrangement.

But, of course, I did hear of Joe again. In fact, a year or so later back in England, I saw his photo on all the book pages above rave reviews for *Catch-22*. In fact, Joseph Heller got even better reviews in Britain than he did in the US. Soon his book became an international bestseller, and its title passed into the language. At the time I was struggling with a second novel and, during blocks, keeping my hand in as a journalist to keep stray wolves from the door. A Sunday paper asked me to interview and write a profile of Joseph Heller who was currently in London. I could have said no, but I had judged a book by the cover and it was payback time. Penance would be good for the soul.

Heller's suite in Claridge's was somewhat more opulent than the slightly flyblown Italian bar on Sixth Avenue where we had had lunch. That was over two years before. He looked a great deal smoother now and was wearing expensive casual clothes. On the coffee table there was an open bottle of champagne in an ice-bucket and several glasses. He offered me one and I declined. I reminded him where we'd last met.

'I knew I knew you from somewhere. Hadn't you written a novel or something?' he said.

'Yes.' I couldn't think of much to add to that.

'It came out?'

'Yes.'

I thought he might ask me how it had done and I could have replied, 'Not quite as well as yours'. But he never asked. Anyway, I was there to interview him. I shouldn't be expecting him to interview me. I started to ask him the questions to which I already knew most of the answers. There had already been a very heavy publicity bombardment for *Catch-22*. The phone interrupted his story about how autobiographical the book was. It was Mike Nichols calling from Hollywood. I knew the film rights had been sold for some astronomic sum. From the phone conversation, it was clear that Mike Nichols was going to direct it. He had recently become one of the top directors on Broadway and in Hollywood. They were talking about the screenplay and clearly getting on well. Heller helped himself to more champagne and motioned to me to help myself. I shook my head. It wasn't the right drink for washing down humble pie.

I wrote the profile without mention of my first meeting with its subject. I managed to struggle through a second novel. Heller had trouble with his second too. The film of *Catch-22* was not a success, but I imagine Joe Heller cried all the way to the bank. I don't begrudge him a cent. *Catch-22* is a terrific book.

I Once Met…

SOPHIA LOREN

I fell in love with Sophia Loren over lunch. We weren't quite alone. She had come to New York to publicise a new film and was with Martin, the Columbia publicist. He was a delightful man I'd met before, thirtyish and fairly openly gay, a courageous thing to be in any major US company at the time. He was also clearly devoted to Sophia Loren, which, after about ten minutes, I found entirely under-standable. She was twenty-four at the time, not beautiful in any regular way, but nonetheless stunning. By Hollywood standards her nose was too long and her hips too big, and she had received considerable publicity for refusing to do anything about either and saying: 'Everything you see I owe to spaghetti.' Pasta never had a better advertisement.

As I was there to write a story about her, I had done my homework. I knew that Loren (née Scicolone) had grown up in Naples in considerable poverty, her father taking off when she was still a baby. She won several beauty compe-titions, went to acting classes in Rome and was an extra in *Quo Vadis*, where she was spotted by the producer, Carlo Ponti. (He was 21 years older than her. He still is and they are still married.) After only five years in films she was a major star in her own country and ready for export.

49

When we had lunch she had been speaking English for about eighteen months. She wasn't fluent, had a strong Neapolitan accent, but had absolutely no problem in understanding or communicating. I remember Martin, an opera-lover, steering the conversation that way. She had had a small role in the film of *Aida* when the eponymous star fell ill. With no singing voice and little knowledge of music, Loren took on the part and learned to mouth all the songs that were sung by Renata Tebaldi. Martin insisted that Italian names were just more musical. Would *Aida* have ever been produced by a George Green? Or the film, if Carlo Ponti was Charlie Bridges?

She had a wonderful, infectious laugh. And was clearly a fine actress. When she said she was sure we would meet again, I actually believed her.

And five years later, I did. By a series of happy coincidences, Sophia starred in *Arabesque*, a film I wrote with Julian Mitchell. The film was a couple of weeks into production when I received an unexpected call from the director, Stanley Donen. I hadn't heard from him since we had finished the script, under his supervision, nine months before. Apparently, Sophia was unhappy with some of the dialogue. Was I available to work on it right away? It was no more than a few days' work; a fee would be arranged with my agent.

I met Stanley Donen at Shepperton where they were shooting some of the interiors. When I arrived he was very preoccupied. He tossed a script at me and briefly explained what Sophia was unhappy about. 'Let's go and talk to her about it.' I had no idea that she was there, but didn't have time to feel nervous. We went to her dressing-room. Five years hadn't made Sophia look any older or less naturally glamorous. She put on a fine show of remembering me. That did my cosmopolitan street cred no harm with the other Stanley. She showed me some of the lines that bothered her. Their rhythm wasn't right for her accent or character. I didn't remember writing those particular lines, but said I'd do my best and went off, inspired, to improve them.

That evening I read through the script and realised it wasn't at all the one that Julian and I had written all those months before. Someone else had clearly been tampering with it. Julian's name and mine were still on the cover. No other name had been added so I suspected that it was Donen himself. I tried to bring it up discreetly with him when I brought my dialogue rewrites back.

'I read it all through. Not quite the script Julian and I wrote.'

'I thought it needed some goosing up so I brought in Peter Stone.'

I was naïvely appalled by the casual assumption that any number of people could tramp through our script without a 'by-your-leave'. Then, just as casually, I could be asked back to rewrite someone else's lines. He didn't seem concerned I might be upset. Though I was still innocent in the ways of Hollywood tycoonery, I did work out that Peter Stone, whoever he was, was obviously too expensive to bring back just for a few lines. I handed over my rewrites. About to go on the set, Stanley didn't look at them. I went and watched him shoot Sophia in a scene with the hero, Gregory Peck, in a hotel bedroom. I couldn't tell whether Sophia was meant to be a goodie or a baddie. She didn't seem too sure either. Afterwards she came over and asked me if I'd done her lines. I nodded and said I hoped she'd like them.

'I'm sure I will,' she said and gave me a radiant smile. And she did say them very nicely in the film. I thought they were quite the best thing in it.

I did meet Sophia again. It was a year later. An adaptation of Romain Gary's *Lady L* was being shot up at Castle Howard, directed by Peter Ustinov. I was a great admirer of Gary's work, but of course the real reason I wanted to write a story about it was to meet Sophia again. She was playing the eponymous heroine who ages from twenty to eighty in the course of the story. When I went into her luxury Winnebago she instantly recognised me. It wasn't so easy for me. It was unfortunately one of the days when she was made up to look eighty, and very convincing it was too. It apparently took three hours to stick on all the latex lines, wrinkles and crow's-feet. I quickly tried to hide the disappointment, but she had spotted it. She laughed – not an octogenarian laugh.

'Aren't you going to kiss me?'

How could I tell friends about this? Sophia Loren had asked me to kiss her and I wasn't that keen on the idea.

I leaned forward and my lips touched the cold, greasy latex of her cheek.

I saw Sophia again recently in Milan. It was on television at the opening of the new La Scala. She is seventy and still looks great. Lucky old Charlie Bridges.

SEX BY NUMBERS

Of course Larkin didn't mean to be taken literally when he wrote 'Sexual intercourse began in 1963', but those of us who were post-pubescent before that date knew what he meant. There didn't seem to be much of that sort of intercourse about, not in books or on the stage, not on the big or small screen, let alone in one's own unmarried life, especially if one was a student. At Cambridge in the fifties, as at most universities, the ratio of male to female students was commonly around ten to one. Ignorance, fear and a terrible shyness, largely based on single-sex education, inhibited both sexes. Unlike this frustrated, silent majority, David Greville was not prepared to wait till 1963 or marriage. Determined to get what he wanted, he believed it was what everyone else wanted too.

So from his rooms in college, just below mine, David strode forth to practise his one-in-ten theory. In this he was certainly helped by being tall and dark with rather saturnine good looks, very much out of the pages of the then hugely popular *Brideshead*. He used what a sex manual would call 'the direct method'. Confronted by any girl who attracted him he would, after some polite conversation, say,

'How about going to bed?' If he'd had enough to drink he abbreviated the message to 'How about a fuck then?' But whether in the polite or the vernacular, it was said with a disarming smile as though proposing a stroll on the Backs. Most of the recipients of this invitation looked initially stunned and then appalled. Most frequently the girls walked away wondering if they'd heard right. But if you believed David and even some of his friends, on occasion the technique actually worked. David claimed a one-in-ten success rate. As he succinctly put it, 'Just make sure you ask ten girls a day – well, maybe not every day.' He was reading English and liked to get a little reading done.

For those of us still trying to shake off the morality and mores of our parents, David was a pioneer and a missionary. Pop hadn't arrived culturally or musically. Jazz was the young person's music, and it was jazz that lured me into a traumatic evening with David. I bumped into him walking slightly unsteadily down King's Parade. When he'd been drinking his behaviour took on a peculiar intensity. He grasped both my arms and announced triumphantly, 'I know where the Jazz Club has gone.' Because of unruly behaviour, the proctors had banned further meetings of the club indefinitely. There were rumours that it had gone underground.

'It's at the Brunswick School – up the Newmarket Road. Got a bike?'

I nodded.

'Let's go. There'll be girls there.'

I knew it was unwise to go anywhere with David in that mood, but I was a jazz fan. I quite liked girls, too. It was also assumed that girls who liked jazz were less inhibited than your average undergraduette. I didn't think David had a bike, but when we met in front of the Senate House a few minutes later he was wobbling around on one. A couple of miles up the Newmarket Road we found the stark, prefabricated building of the Brunswick Primary School.

We parked our bikes just inside the playground. There was no sound of music, but there were lights coming from the building. David must have had special antennae that could sense women at a hundred yards in the dark and through walls. He was already off towards the lights like a sex-starved moth. He reached the double doors ahead of me and swept into the hall just as the music started up. It wasn't jazz. No jazz had ever been written for fifes and bagpipes. As the door closed behind him I saw the poster on it. We were gate-crashing a meeting of the Cambridge University Strathspey and Reel Society. I should have left then but I was mesmerised by the particular eightsome reel unfolding in front of me.

Somewhere, either at public school or deb dances, David had mastered the reel. But tall, thin, pale-faced, in his black, tight-fitting suit, he looked totally out of place among the burly, bekilted Scotsmen. Even the girls, in their white blouses and longer tartan skirts, looked tougher than he did. He bobbed elegantly back and forth. As he twirled round each girl I could see he said a few words to her. It was like watching a multiple Marcel Marceau mime. Each girl, a look of horror on her face, bounced back and then out again to her next male partner. You didn't need to be a lip-reader as four appalled Scots girls told three incredulous Scots men what this filthy English interloper had asked them to come outside and do. David must have been drunker than I thought to put his one-in-ten theory to such a terrible test. At the end of the reel, as the bagpipes gave their final wail, the male members of David's eight-some descended on him as one. He was grabbed, lifted off the floor and raced head-first towards the door. They only half-opened the door as they threw him out, so that he sprawled back into the hall with a bleeding nose. Then they opened the door properly and threw him out again, this time cleanly.

They now came purposefully towards me. I hadn't harassed or propositioned their womenfolk, but was guilty by association. I smiled and gave a what-can-one-do-with-these-drunken-Englishmen shrug. It had some effect because they paused. 'I'll go and see if he's all right.' And with that I went past them fast and out of the door. Outside, David was leaning against a wall, clutching a blood-stained handkerchief to his nose.

'You all right?'

He nodded. 'Wasn't the jazz dub, was it?'

He never referred to that evening again. Exams came and went. We graduated and harsh reality took over. About a year later I bumped into him at a party in London. I had gone there with a girl I was rather keen on. At one point she disappeared for a while and when she re-joined me she looked rather shaken.

'You won't believe this,' she said, 'but that man David you introduced me to – we were standing on the landing talking in front of a cupboard – and suddenly he opened the cupboard and said: "Let's get in here and have a fuck.'"

'You slapped his face?'

'No. There was something about him. A sort of ... little-boy-lost look.'

'Great. So you got in the cupboard.'

'I told him not be silly. Then he said I had to now that he'd asked me. Otherwise he'd be embarrassed.' She seemed far more amused by it all than I was.

I don't know what finally happened to David. I heard he'd become a copywriter in advertising and lived with one of the most attractive girls of our time at Cambridge. Then I heard she had married somebody else. Maybe she'd found him in a cupboard proving his one-in-ten theory. Anyway, I hope he eventually found what he was searching for, in and out of bed, and finally laid his theory to rest.

ON THE TRACK OF
A GOOD STORY

Autumn in New York, late 1950s, and my wife and I had been there long enough to call autumn the fall. Everyone who heard our English accents told us that we must go to New England to see the trees. So we did, and they were right. They were indeed spectacular. As an aspiring journalist, I was always on the lookout for something that would make a good piece. But the trees weren't it. Everyone had written about them. The guidebook even quoted Kipling writing of 'roads paved with crimson and gold', and that was back in 1900.

Then, on our second day, near Springfield, Western Massachusetts, we stumbled on 'Dinosaurland'. It was an open quarry, fronted by a large souvenir shop proclaiming: 'Buy a Dinosaur Track – Petrified Footprints for Moderns – For the Man who has everything. Propr: Carlton S Nash.' It was clearly a quiet day in Dinosaurland as Mr Nash was quickly on to us. He must have detected my British incredulous look. Mr Nash was very passionate about his tracks. They were Triassic, about two hundred and fifty million years old.

He took us to the foot of the quarry and explained that it

had been a dinosaur watering hole. There were sixteen layers of shale, and he had dug most of the tracks out himself. He took us into his shop to show us examples he had varnished and now sold as conversation pieces. They were mostly three-toed tracks looking like large maple-leaves. He said they looked great on a lawn or laid into a patio.

I could hardly ask him if they were genuine, but I did ask what they cost. According to size, one was between $500 and $4,000 (multiply by ten for today). I explained to Mr Nash that we lived in an apartment – no lawn, no patio. But he still pressed his brochure on us. Later, apart from wondering if they really were genuine, my wife and I discussed what sort of conversation you would have with guests after you had shown them your dinosaur track. On the way back to New York, I felt I had a piece coming on, and it started: 'In America you can sell anything – even dinosaur tracks.'

The next thought was that a piece satirising American domestic habits would be more acceptable to a British rather than an American magazine. Then I remembered Malcolm Muggeridge. In an attempt at resuscitation, *Punch* had appointed the controversial journalist and broadcaster as its editor. Dinosaur tracks might be just the conversation piece for Muggeridge.

First I'd better get the facts right. I took myself to the Natural History Museum. The palaeontology curator was very helpful. Dinosaurland's tracks were genuine; they are common in the Connecticut River Valley. It is a Triassic geological area, where the earliest dinosaurs wandered around leaving their hefty footprints as conversation pieces for posterity. There are double profits to be made too. One layer of rock contains the imprint, while the layer above contains a natural cast, and both can be sold.

The phone rang announcing the curator's next visitor. The curator motioned me to stay. 'You must meet him – Leonard Hungerford. He's an Australian concert pianist who collects dinosaur tracks.' Hungerford was a hefty man in his mid-thirties, carrying a large holdall. I was introduced as an Englishman interested in dinosaur tracks. Hungerford greeted me like a kindred spirit. He opened his holdall and produced a small three-toed dinosaur track, his latest find. I listened in awe as they set about the identification. They decided it was a young Coelophysis.

Afterwards I went for coffee with Hungerford. He told me on a recent trip he was digging within a couple of hundred metres of Connecticut jail. A police car arrived. Two police-men got out and asked him what he was doing. 'Digging for dinosaur tracks,' he said. The policemen looked at each other. One got back in the car and Hungerford heard him saying into his radio phone, 'Hey, you heard of guys trying to dig their way out of jail. Well, we've got a nut here trying to dig his way in.' Eventually, Hungerford managed to prove his identity and his sanity.

Back home that evening, I started writing. I airmailed the result to Muggeridge. It was a few weeks before I had a reply. He liked the piece and was going to run it. This would be my first by-line in a British publication.

Hungerford became a good friend. We were invited to his home outside New York, a great jumble of prehistory and music. We went to a recital he gave at Carnegie Hall. On our last visit to his home – we had decided to go back to the UK – he gave us a farewell gift: the young Coelophysis footprint. Naturally, we brought it back with us. Initially we lived in a flat, then another, and neither had a garden or a patio. When we finally moved to a house, our conversation piece had vanished – maybe recognised and taken by a knowledgeable removals man. Millions of years after it had been made in Western Massachusetts, we had lost it in north London. But I still have an LP of Hungerford playing Bach and Beethoven, as well as a copy of the piece that I wrote for Malcolm Muggeridge.

PS I checked and Dinosaurland is still going strong.

Our Chat in Havana

I arrived in Havana at about the same time as Fidel Castro, except that he had to fight his way down from the mountains and I just flew in from New York. I had no ambition to be a war correspondent. I had overlapped with the *Life* reporter who had covered some of the campaign. He was flown home with some nasty tropical illness. I was there to cover another sort of shooting – the filming of Graham Greene's *Our Man in Havana*.

The town was full of Castro's men – though 'men' is not the most accurate description. Everyone armed with a sub-machine seemed to be a long-haired, wispily bearded sixteen-year-old. Castro's rebellion had attracted the youth. Castro himself was then only twenty-nine. After a three-year struggle the vile Batista regime was overthrown and Batista himself made a classic dictator's exit with umpteen billion dollars of public money. Castro was hailed everywhere as a hero – even, briefly, in the US.

Within a few days of Castro coming to power a second invasion arrived – Alec Guinness, Noël Coward, Maureen O'Hara, Ernie Kovacs, the director Carol Reed and Graham Greene himself. Columbia Pictures may have originally done the deal with Batista, but Fidel would honour the contract and guarantee everybody's safety, give or take the odd accidental burst of sub-machine gun fire.

It took time for Castro to clear Havana of its corrupt, capitalist legacy. The luxury hotel where Peter Stackpole, the *Life* photographer, and I stayed was still owned and run by Florida *mafiosi*. Its casino still flourished and, at an outside ring of tables, expensive-looking prostitutes had their well-established pitches. The first night Peter and I went out for a late-night dinner. We followed the sound of a voice shouting and hectoring and found ourselves in the main square. There were about 20,000 people there and above them on a balcony Fidel himself, haranguing them cincuenta to the dozen. We eventually found the recommended restaurant. After a leisurely dinner we retraced our steps. It was around two in the morning when we found ourselves back in the main square. There were still about 20,000 people there, though perhaps not the same 20,000, and Fidel was still up on his balcony haranguing them.

I had read nearly all Greene's books and he was my literary hero. One evening, down by the port, I found myself standing next to him watching a scene being shot. I realised then that I was not a born journalist. Greene was most affable; I found myself tongue-tied. Watching a film being shot, John Mortimer once said, was about as exciting as watching your toenails grow. Greene obviously felt that way too. He suggested we go and have a drink.

We found a bar and I discovered Greene had an amazing capacity for putting one at ease. Instead of my interviewing him I found I was doing the talking. Greene had visited

Cuba once before – in the bad old days, which were, after all, only a fortnight before. He said Havana used to be famous for its exhibitions, one of the best-known of which was Superman, named for his huge endowment. Greene had heard that Superman had gone underground. Did I know anything about this?

For a moment it occurred to me that maybe this was why Greene was being so affable. Mistaking me for a born journalist, he thought I was just the man who would know the whereabouts of Superman. It was an unworthy thought.

Greene seemed no less friendly when I admitted my ignorance. He suggested we go in search of Superman. The idea that this phenomenon would take his massive member 'underground' was surreal enough without my going in search of it with a famous British novelist. But if I backed out now what sort of a journalist would I be?

Greene's Spanish was good, and he told various taxi-drivers what we were in search of. They all nodded knowledgeably and we did end up at a series of exhibitions, but they were all above ground and only featured women, though impressively endowed. I found them all fairly revolting. Greene seemed to find the whole experience mildly amusing. I realised that that was how I must be if I was going to be a successful novelist.

Next day I was having a haircut in the hotel's barber shop. The manicurist there was a prototypical Cuban beauty in her late twenties. Unlikely as it was, I was convinced that I knew her from somewhere. It turned out that till a fortnight before she had worked in the hairdresser's on West 48th Street where I sometimes had my hair cut. She had just returned to live with her family in the new Cuba. Her name was Conchita. She was starstruck and begged me to take her to see some of the filming. I agreed to get her into the casino that night where we were photographing a scene being shot.

I didn't think it would look very professional to be seen escorting so startling an example of local talent while working, so I placed Conchita at a table and ordered her a drink. Work meant seeing that Peter Stackpole took the right pictures. As *Life* photographers invariably took the right pictures it wasn't a very onerous job. Afterwards I joined Conchita, ordered another round and told her about the film. We were interrupted by Graham Greene. He was all affability. I introduced him to Conchita. He sat down and insisted on ordering more drinks.

Whether Conchita knew who he was or not, she was clearly fascinated by him. He asked her the most personal questions in the most casual but sincere way and she responded without embarrassment. Within ten minutes he had discovered that she had had to leave Cuba because she was pregnant by a married man. She had lived in New York as a single mother. Now she was back, all was forgiven, and her little daughter was being looked after by her family. I marvelled at his ability to charm bilingually and felt about as necessary to this meeting of minds as I did to Peter taking his highly professional photos. Greene at least had the grace to turn to me quietly at one moment and say, 'I hope I'm not, er, interrupting anything.' It was my opportunity to tell him to bugger off and go look for Superman. But I didn't. A few minutes later I excused myself and left them together. When I saw him a couple of days later Conchita was not referred to.

When my first novel came out I sent Greene a copy. He wrote me a kind and complimentary letter back. The following year, back in London, I couldn't resist the temptation to enter a *New Statesman* competition to write the opening of Greene's as yet unpublished new novel. Apparently they ran this competition every few years and Greene invariably won it himself under a pseudonym. That year I won it, all of five guineas, and Greene came third. I wonder if it wasn't, subconsciously, my revenge for Conchita.

DAVID NIVEN

David Niven holds the record for the shortest performance ever to win the Oscar for best actor. It was in 1958, and he was on screen for only twenty-five minutes in the film adaptation of Terence Rattigan's *Separate Tables*. Niven played the bogus Major Pollock, living in a residential seaside hotel and trying to prevent his stuffy co-residents from seeing the local newspaper. It carried the news that he had just been charged with harassing young women in a local cinema. It was a deeply moving performance, all the more surprising as Niven, the most popular British actor in Hollywood, was best known for playing smooth comedy parts.

Shortly after winning his Oscar, Niven was invited to one of Henry Luce's monthly *Life* magazine lunches. As with Marilyn, as a junior reporter I was sent to collect and escort the guest to lunch. The editor probably also thought that, as *Life*'s token Englishman, I would get on well with Niven. I did a little homework and went off to collect him from the Waldorf.

Because we are so used to seeing them on a big screen, film actors seem surprisingly small in the flesh. Niven was no exception, but he did stand very straight. This, along with his neat moustache and immaculate turn-out, clearly spelled out his earlier background. He had been at Sandhurst, commissioned in the Rifle Corps and had a distinguished war record. His immediate charm and friend-liness felt genuine and not a celebrity PR act. In the taxi, however, he admitted to mild stage fright about meeting Henry Luce. What was he like? I couldn't help Niven there. I had once travelled alone with Luce up thirty floors in a lift but he had not uttered even a 'Hi'. He was known as a serious man and, reputedly, not many people made him laugh. I didn't tell Niven that, but he decided he needed a stiff drink before lunch.

He stopped the taxi at the 21, one of Manhattan's smartest restaurants and bars. Inside, he was treated like royalty. Our drinks appeared in a flash. The barman was a very old friend. When Niven first came to New York, he had worked briefly as a whisky salesman, and the 21 had been among his clients. Fortunately, we had a little time on our hands and had a chance to talk. Niven turned out to be a marvellous raconteur. When I asked him if he had ever acted on stage, he positively lit up. I had obviously pressed the right button. Yes, he had even acted on Broadway – but only once. He had played Gloria Swanson's lover in an ill-fated French comedy. Unfortunately, she had designed her own costumes and on the opening night, in the first scene, he embraced her too energetically. Somewhere from the depths of her corset a whalebone twanged, came loose and flew up his nostril. Niven froze and forgot his lines. He demonstrated all this brilliantly, ending with a cocktail stick up his nostril. He quoted a line from Walter Kerr's review in the *Herald Tribune*: 'Like the play, Miss Swanson's clothes fell apart in the first act.' Niven never acted on stage again. Miss Swanson did, but gave up designing her clothes.

We just made it to the Time-Life dining room, but before we went in he said, 'If I dry with Mr Luce, ask me that question about the theatre.' Inside, I was meant to sit at the end of the table but Niven insisted I sat opposite him. The silence Niven dreaded didn't come until the dessert. Niven shot me a dramatic glance. I cleared my throat: 'Before making films, did you ever act in the theatre?' 'I wish you hadn't asked me that question,' he said, giving me a disarming smile. 'Yes. I even acted on Broadway – but only once,' and he was off. It was a word-perfect performance. This time it was the end of a teaspoon instead of a cocktail stick he put up his nostril. And Luce was laughing.

When Niven was leaving, he took my arm and said quietly, 'You gave that cue beautifully.' He made me feel I had just won an Oscar for best supporting actor. I never saw Niven again, except on screen. He made another dozen or so successful films but never won another award. Between films he wrote a memoir, *The Moon's a Balloon*, that became a number one bestseller.

WON OVER BY WOODY

Woody Allen has now been writing and directing his own films for fifty years. He has also acted in many of them. His new film, *Magic in the Moonlight*, which opened in July, is his forty-fifth. Not all of them are to everyone's taste. As the last line – Billy Wilder's, not Woody Allen's – in *Some Like it Hot* says, 'Nobody's poifect'. But for me, even Woody's less-successful films are light-years better than the comedies that currently roll out of Hollywood – or Britain. My most recent favourite was the joyful and literate *Midnight in Paris*, which, in 2012, won Woody his second Oscar for best screenplay. He has won several for direction and best film. Yet whether his latest wins any awards or not – he thinks awards are 'silly' and doesn't go to the ceremonies anyway – Woody Allen will be undeterred. He has already started making his next film – and on 1st December he will be seventy-nine.

I must admit, however, to some proprietary feeling about Woody. I didn't personally discover him, but I was there in Hollywood when it happened – and so was Godfrey Winn. In the mid-sixties, Winn was reputedly the highest-paid journalist in Fleet Street, his only rival the slightly more up-market Beverley Nichols. They both wrote syrupy columns for the tabloids and for mass-circulation women's magazines. Both were discreetly gay: their predominant appeal was to middle-class, middle-aged women who had no idea their Fleet Street heroes were not handsome heterosexuals.

Godfrey and I had been invited to be the two British journalists to report on the seventieth birthday celebrations for Jack, the elder of the Warner Brothers, in Hollywood. Godfrey was in his late fifties, very fit and shiny-looking. He had been both a juvenile actor and a talented tennis player – the south of England junior champion – and had ended up coaching guests at Somerset Maugham's Cap Ferrat villa. Maugham had encouraged his literary ambitions and the two novels Godfrey subsequently wrote were published successfully. During the war he had hair-raising experiences as an ordinary seaman on the Murmansk convoys to northern Russia: afterwards he wrote a book about them and resumed his climb up Fleet Street's greasy pole. He had the gift of talking about himself without coming across as grand. Unlike your true egocentric, he did ask questions. He discovered I'd worked for four years in America, had a wife, a child and a recently published novel. He confided that he was pathetically nervous about going to Hollywood – 'You will stick by me, won't you?'

On our first morning we were taken on a tour of the Warner Bros studios and to a screening of their new film, *The Great Race*, a feeble rip-off of *Around the World in Eighty Days*. Afterwards, at a reception with the director and cast, we paid the price one pays for a freebie – the set smile and the false compliment. Limpet-like, Godfrey stuck to me as though I was some streetwise Los Angelino, even though I'd never been to LA before. We went to several other parties. We were not introduced to any lovely Hollywood starlets. I sensed that our hosts thought we were a couple. The next evening a limo took us both to the vast studio where they were holding the birthday dinner for Jack Warner.

A spry-looking seventy with a slim-line moustache, Warner was surrounded by an A to Z of famous Hollywood faces. There was lavish entertainment and verbal tributes, the food and drink unlimited. Towards the end of the floorshow the MC asked for 'a big hand for a new comedian who is going places'. A small, incredibly twitchy young man with reddish hair came on and was introduced as Mr Woody Allen. Clearly no one had ever heard of him and the audience seemed to catch a sort of sympathetic nervousness. After a few stammering lines with an occasional clicking noise he made with his tongue as if for punctuation, he launched himself into a monologue: 'I shot a moose one day – in upstate New York. I strapped it on my fender...' But Woody's shot had only stunned the moose and it revives driving through the Holland Tunnel. To get rid of it, Woody takes it to a fancy-dress party he's been invited to.

I suddenly had a tingling feeling up my spine: this nervous, nebbishy little guy in his T-shirt and crumpled suit had take-off and was flying. And the Hollywood greats were going with him. His moose was now at the party, mixing freely. 'At midnight there's a competition for best costume. The first prize goes to the Berkowitzes, a married couple dressed as a moose. The moose comes second. The moose is furious. They lock antlers and knock each other unconscious. This is my chance. I grab the moose, strap him on my fender and drive off – but I've got the Berkowitzes. So I'm driving along with two Jewish people strapped to my fender...'

That night I knew that Woody Allen was here to stay. Godfrey didn't find him that funny – 'not my cup of tea'. There would always be some people like that. Next morning he thanked me for looking after him so well and flew off to join friends in the Caribbean. I flew back to Muswell Hill. We kept in touch and had a couple of lunches together, the Hollywood experience a bizarre bond. He had a tennis court at his Sussex home and asked me down to play. A few days before I was due there he died of a heart attack on court. It was 1971, the year Woody made *Everything You Always Wanted to Know About Sex* (*But were afraid to ask*). I doubt if that would have been Godfrey's cuppa either.

A SERGEANT'S TALE

It is well over fifty years since the last intake of healthy over-eighteen males was called up for National Service. So if you can remember your army number and rank (22344998 Sergeant Price, S.) you're still, at least mentally, in good shape. Worth remembering, because that was all you had to volunteer if captured by the enemy (Geneva Convention, 1929). I can remember a lot of the rest too, as if it was yesterday – in fact often much better than yesterday.

I don't want to pull rank, but let me just explain the sergeant bit. After many victories and defeats, I was sent to Wilton Park, Beaconsfield, the HQ of the Royal Army Educational Corps, for a three-month course to become an Educational Corps sergeant. At the induction talk an officer informed us that most people didn't know what the RAEC on our new shoulder flashes stood for. When told they'd say, 'Like the Intelligence Corps, eh?' – to which we should reply, 'No, we're more intelligent – and much older.' Apparently the corps was pre-Crimean War, founded in 1845 as the Corps of Army Schoolmasters, when they had mostly taught reading and writing. Some of us, if we passed the course, might find ourselves doing the same – there was still fifteen per cent illiteracy in the army. I learned later that the corps' proudest battle honour was the General Election of 1945. The influence of left-leaning, wartime education sergeants was thought to have helped turn out Churchill and bring in Attlee.

On the parade ground we were a fairly motley group from different regiments – artillery bombardiers with poor aim, claustrophobic tank troopers, infantry privates who were always out of step. There were university graduates, others en route to university, and a fair sprinkling of O- and A-levels among the rest. We weren't exactly a crack body of men, but we weren't stupid. An Irish Guards sergeant-major had something to say about that on our first parade. 'Some of youse may think this course is going to be a doddle. It won't be,' he roared at us. But, clearly a cultivated man, he'd gone sixteen words without the common expletive. He continued: 'Some of youse may leave here as teachers, but first and fucking foremost you'll leave here as soldiers.'

Inevitably, our hut of eight had a know-all. Private Lewis knew we'd be turned into soldiers by sadistic Guards NCOs while RAEC officers turned us into teachers, all under the command of a 'nutter' with one eye, who sometimes wore a dress. Next day we assembled to meet him. Major Lord Wavell MC of the Black Watch had two eyes but only one arm, and he wore the dark green tartan kilt of his regiment. He was thick-set, of medium height, with gingery hair and a belligerent square jaw, and, if a nutter, he was a formid-ably tough one. I learned later that he had lost his arm and won his Military Cross in the Burma campaign. He told us what was in store if we passed the course – attachment to a regiment or corps, holding our own in a sergeants' mess with men fifteen or twenty years older than us, who had probably served in the war, some of whom we might be teaching. We had only three months to learn a hell of a lot.

Wavell's teaching was, by military standards, highly eccentric. He talked about the Greeks, their ideal of 'excellence', and their military and political virtues. Later, he moved onto T E Lawrence and his *Seven Pillars of Wisdom*. What did he want of us? Were we to become soldier-scholars, 'excellent' in body and soul? Next, he introduced us to the war poets, Brooke, Graves and Sassoon. He read us the last lines of Wilfred Owen's 'Dulce et decorum est':

> My friend, you would not tell with such high zest
> To children ardent for some desperate glory,
> The old lie: Dulce et decorum est
> Pro patria mori.

It sounded strange coming from the mouth of a decorated war hero, whose even more decorated father had been a field marshal.

Then it was up and away – an initiative test. We were each given a pound, a map and told to meet up at a youth hostel in the Lake District within thirty-six hours. Once there, it was four days of exhausting hikes from hostel to hostel with mountains in between. There was a Cumbrian in my group of four who knew all the bus routes and best pubs, but on the third day we made a fatal mistake. Wavell had led the first group, but we managed to arrive before them at the next hostel – and he hadn't noticed us overtaking. Next day he led our group – up Helvellyn. His conversation was fascinating – ours ran out at around five hundred feet above sea-level. At least fifteen years older than us, Wavell got to the summit first. He stood there in his kilt, looking down at us as we gasped up the final slope, not like valiant Greeks or rugged soldier-scholars, just four shattered skivers who'd been caught out.

Amidst all the brutal soldiering we were actually learning how to teach. My own teaching practice hadn't gone that well, and as I hadn't won the MC on the Lake District campaign, I worried about passing the course. Private Know-all Lewis knew that borderliners should put their names down for the boxing competition, as Wavell was impressed by 'a good scrapper'.

I'd never boxed before, but I'd seen newsreels of Joe Louis, the world champ, and our local hero, Freddie Mills. I'd just imitate them, guard up, bounce from foot to foot, then a lethal upper-cut and a fast cross. I felt pretty confident when I climbed into the ring. My opponent, Private Radcliffe, was exactly my height and weight. He'd never boxed before either, and we agreed there was no point in killing each other. He must have seen the newsreels too, as in the first round we danced around, doing everything professionals do, except throwing hard punches. I could see Wavell, in the front row, wasn't impressed.

Early in the next round Radcliffe lowered his guard. It was now or never, or we'd both stay privates till demob. A good, clean knock-out was the most painless ending. My lethal upper-cut found his jaw, but iron-man Radcliffe just swayed slightly and then hit me full on the nose. Christ, it hurt! My eyes watered. Wavell would think I was crying. I staggered into a clinch and held on. 'Sorry,' Radcliffe whispered, 'but I want to pass too.' The next six minutes were a painful blur. The fight was declared a draw. I was sore all over for a week, but I passed the course – and so did Radcliffe.

About two thirds of us passed, and we stood to attention on the parade ground with our stripes newly sewed on. The RAEC had no regimental band of its own, but Wavell's masterstroke was to borrow, for the occasion, the Black Watch Pipe and Drum Band. A sergeant-major screamed an order, pipes piped, drums were drummed, and led by Wavell, kilt swinging, we marched up the long drive of Wilton Park towards Beaconsfield church for the passing-out service. To march behind a pipe and drum band is an extraordinary experience. It actually made me feel, in the memorable words of that Irish CSM, 'first and fucking foremost a soldier'.

Wavell wasn't someone you forgot, or ever expected to see again. Yet in my second term at Cambridge I came back to my rooms and found him ensconced in an armchair. He explained that he often looked up his Beaconsfield alumni. He remembered I'd gone to an Ordnance Corps depot to teach illiterates. He wanted to know how I was getting on with the illiterates at Cambridge and what periods of history I was doing. I'd always thought he was a frustrated academic, and asked if he'd ever thought of it. 'Not for me,' he said. 'Not got the patience. Army in my blood, I'm afraid.' He told me of his great triumph in finally winning his battle with the War Office to be allowed to re-join his regiment: 'I'm more use with one arm than...' He smiled at me and left to see another Beaconsfield alumnus.

On Christmas Eve 1953, I was at home listening to the news and the last item was: 'The War Office has just announced the death of Major Archibald, Earl Wavell, MC in Kenya. He was killed leading a patrol of his regiment, the Black Watch, against a group of Mau Mau terrorists. Earl Wavell was thirty-five.'

SERENDIPITY IN
KENTISH TOWN

I've always liked the sound of the word 'serendipity'. The *Compact Oxford* defines it as 'the occurrence of events by chance in a beneficial or lucky way'. That makes it different from its cousin, coincidence, which has chance events occurring but no beneficial effects. It is the outcome that decides which is which. Which of them was it that brought me, James Joyce and the Northern line (High Barnet branch) together? It was about four years ago. I was coming back from town on the Tube, and was fascinated by the elegant-looking man sitting opposite me. He was sixtyish, tall, silver-haired, with a well-trimmed beard and moustache, very rare in these days of deep five o'clock shadow. But the most distinctive thing about him was his colour-coordination. The theme was red, nothing Santa Claus-garish, but different shades for his socks, tweed trousers, shirt, jumper and jacket. Not to be over the top, his shoes were sensibly brown. He certainly didn't seem a City type, but he was reading the *Financial Times*. When not distracted by my fellow-traveller's shades of red, I was reading Joyce's *Dubliners*.

Just after Euston, the man lowered his paper, leaned

forward, and gestured at my book. 'Great stories, aren't they?' I was taken aback that somebody, clearly not deranged, would talk to me on a London Tube. Maybe he was Irish. There was a pause before I said 'Yes.'

'Have you read much Joyce?' He didn't sound Irish – in fact, he had no noticeable accent.

'Yes, quite a bit.'

'*Ulysses*?'

'Oh, yes.'

'Great novel.'

'Absolutely.'

'More fun than this,' he waved his *Financial Times* at me. 'How about *Finnegans Wake*?'

'Started but couldn't finish.'

'Try again,' he said, 'Think of it as music.' And with that he stood up. The train was stopping. It was Kentish Town, and the man in red got off. I didn't have the presence of mind to run after him, to ask him how he had come to Joyce, what he did for a living, let alone where he bought his clothes. Now I would never know. And he would never know that I was, in fact, reading *Dubliners* for at least the second time, and currently having a Joyce crisis.

My own connection with Joyce went back a long way. I had spent part of my childhood in Dublin. In the summer I would be taken to Sandycove, and swam in the shadow of the Joyce Tower. I remember asking my father why the Martello tower was named after a girl. He explained that Joyce was no girl, but a great Irish writer who had stayed there briefly in 1904. The opening scene of his great book *Ulysses* started there. What's more, he said with some pride,

the hero of the book was Leopold Bloom, a Dublin Jew.
Because my family were Dublin Jews, there had been much
speculation in that small community about who had been
the model for Bloom. There were several suspects. I only
discovered the genuine model for Bloom many years later
when I read Italo Svevo's *Confessions of Zeno*, rightly considered one of the twentieth century's great comic novels.
It was published in 1926 but, like *Ulysses*, only after many
setbacks. The book is set in Trieste, where Svevo was born
and bred. I read more about Svevo and found out that he
had known Joyce there.

In 1904, intent on becoming a writer, Joyce had exiled
himself from Ireland. He had answered a newspaper
advertisement and found himself a job teaching English in
the Berlitz language school in Trieste. Three years later, a
42-year-old businessman, Ettore Schmitz, came to Berlitz
for English lessons. He was given Joyce as his teacher –
definitely serendipity. Schmitz was Jewish and worked for
a family firm which made a marine paint that protected
ships' hulls, and he needed better English in order to do
business with the British Admiralty. He had also written
two unsuccessful novels under the name Italo Svevo. He
took the name, he explained, 'out of pity for the one
vowel surrounded by six consonants in the name Schmitz'.
Schmitz/Svevo and Joyce soon discovered they were both
writers. They read and admired each other's unsuccessful
work, became lifelong friends and were an enormous help
to each other. And I discovered that Bloom was modelled
on – inspired by would be a more accurate word, not on a
Dublin Jew – Joyce didn't know any – but a Triestine one.

The Perse Players' production of *Hamlet* (1949): Peter Hall (front of stage) as Hamlet; Stanley (centre, with crown) as the Player King.

'Now might I do it pat': Peter Hall as Hamlet, poised to kill Claudius.

Hackney Downs School production of *Macbeth* (1947): Harold Pinter as Macbeth.

Dr Norman Haire, President of the Sex Congress of Geneva.

Archibald, Lord Wavell: inspirational, terrifying, and Stanley's CO in the Education Corps.

Opposite: Lady Jeanne Campbell: stepdaughter of the Duchess of Argyll, and mistress of Kennedy, Krushchev and Castro.

Margaret, Duchess of Argyll, in *femme fatale* pose.

Photoshoot for *Town* magazine, 1964:
Mandy Rice-Davies as Fanny Hill;
Stanley as elderly hair fetishist.

Caravans (1978): Anthony Quinn as Zorba the Afghan.

Noël Coward and friend, Havana,
March 1959.

Graham Greene in Havana,
March 1959.

Joyce was to pick Svevo's brains about all things Jewish.

With a twenty-year age gap between them, they made an odd couple. One tall and thin, the other smaller and rounder, both multilingual polymaths. Each had a family, Svevo a wife and daughter, Joyce a partner, Nora Barnacle, a son and a daughter. Joyce was a heavy drinker, Svevo a heavy smoker, Joyce a constant borrower and, fortunately for him, Svevo was a generous lender.

I always intended to try to write about this fruitful friendship. The idea stayed in the back of my mind, but other writing kept intervening. Then, finally, I ran out of excuses. I had to make a start. I started reading – and reading. The only thing I didn't do was write. I became daunted by the material, a not uncommon condition among writers: if you keep on researching, you might even avoid writing altogether. That was the state I was in when I met the man in red. About a week after that, I took the Northern line into town. I was reading Edna O'Brien's slim but excellent biography of Joyce and came across a marvellous quote in one of his letters. He was writing to his benefactress, Harriet Weaver, a millionaire with a puritanical streak. He was worried that she might hear about his recent carousing in Zurich. It was all wild gossip, he wrote. 'A batch of people here tried to induce me to enter a sanatorium where a certain Doctor Jung (the Swiss Tweedledum who is not to be confused with the Viennese Tweedledee) amuses himself at the expense of ladies and gentlemen with bees in their bonnet.'

I got off the train at Leicester Square with Edna O'Brien in my pocket, and was confronted by a film poster for

A Dangerous Method. The strapline over the title read 'Two great minds in conflict'. There were pictures of two faintly familiar faces, and under them were critics' quotes: 'Michael Fassbender is magnificent as Carl Jung' and 'Freud is brought wonderfully to life by Viggo Mortensen'. There was also a picture of Keira Knightley, obviously the woman 'the two great minds' were in conflict over. I stared at the poster. Maybe my hair stood on end. Was someone trying to tell me something? Joyce believed in epiphanies, those moments that bring a sudden understanding. Had I just had two, in the space of a week, on the Northern line? Should I dismiss them as meaningless chance or did they mean more? It was up to me to decide. Next day I started writing. I like to think it was Jung, Freud and the Man in Red who helped turn mere coincidence into serendipity.

Larry, Ireland and
St George

During the war my mother and I were sent to neutral Dublin to stay with my grandparents. Going to 'the pictures' there was my weekly treat, but on one occasion my treat was to be allowed to cycle, with an older cousin, to Powerscourt, a stately home fourteen miles outside Dublin. I was told Laurence Olivier was shooting *Henry V* there, though neither of those names meant much to me then. I wasn't too sure about 'shooting' either.

It turned out to be something very chaotic. There were lots of men in armour who kept mounting their horses, getting them in line, and then some of them would fall off. Various men, in ordinary clothes, kept shouting at them through loudspeakers. Meanwhile, a knowledgeable spectator next to us explained the story so far – not the story of *Henry V*, but of what was happening in front of us. Apparently without enough manpower available in wartime Britain for the battle of Agincourt, they had come to Ireland to shoot it. They had tried to recruit their 'extras' from farmers and members of the local hunts, but when news got out what an 'extra' was paid daily there were long

queues of very questionable-looking individuals lining up
to play French knights.

The shooting was usually all right in the mornings, but
after lunch, after they'd taken 'a few jars' – our informant
winked at us – weren't they falling off their horses, and
didn't that damage and dirty the armour, which, after all,
was only made of cardboard and had to be repaired, and
didn't that all take time? He gave us another wink – on their
pay as extras, wasn't that no bad thing? He told the story
gleefully, turning it into a tale of the Irish, albeit disguised
as French knights, outwitting and defeating the English at
this particular Agincourt. He pointed at a distraught-looking man in a raincoat standing on a wooden platform near
the 'knights' – 'That's yer man Oliver. He's the director,
poor bugger.'

We spent most of the afternoon there, but never saw one
complete charge where something didn't go wrong, as our
winking informant had predicted. The payroll for extras
was clearly soaring, and that was even before the English
bowmen, no doubt the Irish in disguise again, came on the
scene.

A year later, back in London, the war not quite over,
Henry V was playing at a nearby cinema, the Astoria,
Finsbury Park. For some unaccountable reason, the Astoria
was modelled on the Alhambra in Granada, with fountains
in the foyer, and a dark, domed ceiling with stars twinkling
in it. I was still on my parental ration of one film a week.
On that occasion my parents might even have come with
me.

I don't remember anything about that day except the film

itself. I was entranced from the first moment when that piece of manuscript paper floats down out of a blue sky to the accompaniment of William Walton's music, and swirls into the open wooden circle of the Globe Theatre. I didn't know the play and it was a wonder to me.

And then it came to the Battle of Agincourt. I couldn't believe what I saw. From a shower of drunken or hungover Irish farmers and labourers in fields fourteen miles outside Dublin, that distraught-looking man in a raincoat on a wooden platform had created one of the – no, not one of, but the greatest cavalry charge ever filmed, and one of the most inspiring battle scenes ever. He himself was a great Henry V, Shakespeare was a great writer, and Walton a great composer. I came out of that exotic cinema hooked on the miracle of film and all that it could do. It had the effect on me it was meant to have on the entire population at that stage of the war – a belief that the English, demoralised, weary, outnumbered and fighting on foreign soil, would always be victorious in the end. And, most fortunately, this time they were again.

The film was nominated for an Oscar, but never won an award. I always felt I wanted to thank Olivier personally for introducing me to Shakespeare, to great acting and to what films could do at their best. More than forty years later I had that opportunity.

Once a year the Dramatists' Club hold a dinner at the Garrick Club and invite a distinguished guest. In 1988 they invited Olivier. They had left the invitation sadly late as he had stopped acting and was in poor health. We saw just how poor when he arrived. He looked incredibly frail and had warned the Club that he was not up to making an after-dinner speech, but his great friend Anthony Quayle would speak for him.

Quayle did so graciously and was loudly applauded. Everyone then turned to applaud Olivier separately. He suddenly looked very sad, the look of a man who had finally let his audience down. Very slowly he got to his feet. The once strong and totally distinctive voice was very weak, but as he spoke it grew in volume, the old cadences came back, his shoulders straightened, the words came out eloquent and clear. I can't remember any of them, but it was a magnificent performance. There was defiance in his voice, as if to tell us that if he were going to die he'd rather do it on stage playing to a full house. He sat down slowly and there wasn't a dry eye in the house.

Somehow it didn't seem quite the moment to go up and thank him for *Henry V*.

In Search of Il Duce

The coach picked us up in Milan and headed north to Lake Como, our first trip to the Italian Lakes. The scenery was stunning, but I was glad to leave the driving to someone else. The narrow road snaking along the western shore of Como was scarcely wide enough for two cars to pass, let alone two coaches. The Italian woman guide told us that if we looked down to our right we would see the top of George Clooney's lakeside villa. Everybody looked. A little later she told us to look at the small road to the left. It led up to the village of Mezzegra, where, on 28 April 1945, Mussolini and his mistress, Clara Petacci, had been executed by the partisans. Our guide didn't realise till someone shouted out that today was the 28th April. It was a strange frisson – just happening to pass on the sixty-sixth anniversary of Il Duce's death. I looked in our guidebook. It mentioned that Mussolini had spent his last night in a private house in the village, but said no more. Later I asked our guide if there was any memorial there. She had never been there and didn't know. She shook her head sadly, 'Those were terrible times here'.

I had studied history at university and it didn't feel right

just to settle for George Clooney's roof and to 'ooh' and
'ahh' at the beauties of the lake and mountains. The least I
could do was find and photograph an important and lurid
piece of twentieth-century history. It was mildly embarrassing asking at the hotel desk about Mussolini, but no one
there knew anything about a memorial. A couple of days
later my wife and I set out for Mezzegra. We took a boat
two stops down the lake, and disembarked to find ourselves
on the traffic-packed lakeside road. We walked along it with
buses and lorries brushing past us, and then, with relief,
found an arrow pointing to a 'green route' up to Mezzegra.
It started as a very steep climb and then got steeper. There
were stunning views, but we hadn't the breath to 'ooh' and
'ahh'. It was hot too. My wife Judy, who hadn't studied
history at college, said, with considerable sub-text, 'How
much further?'

I had the map. 'We're over halfway now,' I lied.

'There'll probably be nothing there,' she said encourag-
ingly.

We finally reached the outskirts of the village. A youngish
couple, who looked to be locals, were walking towards us.
In my halting Italian I asked if they knew the memorial to
Mussolini. 'No. We're Dutch,' they replied in good English.
We pressed on and found the local church. On the steps in
front of it were two elderly men definitely talking in Italian.
Again I went into my '*C'é un memoriale a Mussolini qui?*' I
thought they looked at me suspiciously before one of them
nodded and went into staccato Italian. I didn't understand
more than '*a sinistra*' and '*alla destra*'. I'd have been smarter
to speak to him in slow English. Fortunately his excellent

gesticulation made it clear there was something down the hill to the left and then right down a zigzag street.

With a shower of *grazie milles* and *pregos*, we set off. However, none of the elderly man's gestures had indicated how far it was. We were almost giving up when we saw a small roadside sign that read '*Fatto storica*. Site of Historical Event'. Fifty metres further on, fixed to the stone gatepost of an ordinary family house, was a black wooden cross and on it the words 'Benito Mussolini, 28 Aprile, 1945'. As I took a photo or two a passing car tooted its horn. It was a couple in a four-wheel drive. The driver seemed to wave at me.

Judy said, 'Did you see what he did?'

'He waved.'

'No, he didn't. He gave the Fascist salute.'

'No. I think it was that Dutch couple we met.'

'The Dutch don't give Fascist salutes.'

As neither of us had seen the number-plate of the car, our disagreement went unresolved. Coming back down the hill we had the breath to 'ooh' and 'aah' at the beauty of the lake, the mountains and the villages.

A week later at home the pictures looked even better on our computer screen. I remembered that Mezzegra wasn't the end of the Mussolini story and I googled his death and found a YouTube film of the street we had walked down, the sign and the discreet black cross on the gate. We needn't have tired ourselves out climbing, exhausting my Italian and taking the pictures. Another click on YouTube and we'd moved on to some extraordinary contemporary footage of the bodies of Mussolini, Clara Petacci and five other Fascisti being hung up by their ankles at an Esso station on the Piazzale Loreto in Milan. A huge crowd had gathered to watch and shout.

Of course nowadays you don't have to go anywhere any more. You can stay home and see everything on television or your computer screen. Still, I was glad we'd had the experience of that very steep hill and of taking our own pictures. And something the internet and YouTube will never be able to tell us is whether it was a Fascist salute, or just a friendly Dutch wave.

TALES FROM A BALLY

The maps and road-signs of Ireland are covered with Bally-this and Bally-that. The word simply means town in Irish, though it is doubtful if the vast majority of Ballys were ever more than a few houses, possibly a church, and probably a bar. For purposes of privacy I'll call our bally Ballybackofbeyond. It is in East Cork and we don't want it to suffer the fate of West Cork, now choked with traffic all summer and, at all seasons, with the second homes of foreign industrialists and show-biz persons and the expensive bistros that feed them. Ballybacketc is not really our Bally, though we – my wife and I – have been going there for years because some good friends there lend us their barn. It no longer contains their animals and has all mod cons. It's a good place to write, read and walk along the cliff-top, but better still, it's a great place to listen. Like most Ballys, ours is full of storytellers, and their stories are by no means parochial – not in the least.

For example, take Gerald's story, heard on my second morning there. I'm trying to take a photo of a fine-looking but camera-shy goat in a neighbour's field when Gerald's car skids to a halt beside me. He bounds out of the car to give me a hug. The Irish are more uninhibited in their greetings than the English. Gerald is a spry man in his late fifties, tanned by the Ethiopian sun. He spends three months a year in Addis Ababa and is just back. He used to own a good second-hand bookshop in Cork, but gave it up to sell books from home and devote more time to his calling. He has discovered Ethiopia and, in particular, the Mother Teresa Hospice for the Homeless and Destitute, which he uses as a base for organising educational and self-help programmes for young people. I'd heard that this year he has single-handedly raised £16,000 locally. The brochure for this one-man mission emphasises 'No Corruption, Third Party or Overheads – I meet all my own expenses.'

Sitting in his car, he tells me about the 20,000 pairs of plastic shoes he has just distributed and then about how the nuns decided he should visit some of the people he had helped in their own homes. They lent him the mission car and their driver, Bushey – 'a grand old man, bilingual, thank God. The first house we go into they give me a grand greeting. Bushey explains that now I must accept their hospitality and eat with them. There was a powerful smell in there, I can tell you. I asked Bushey what it was. "Boiled onion," he says. "It's the traditional dish. You have to eat one." "Nothing else?" "No, they are poor people." I ask him how many homes we are visiting. "Eight," says he. "I can't." "You must, or they'll be very offended." Then I had this great idea. "Tell them I'm fasting." Poor old Bushey shook his head, looked downcast. "It is not a fast day. You are not fasting. You want me to tell a lie?" "Yes." "I cannot lie to them. It is a sin." "Yes, but it will be my sin. I accept the responsibility. Think of it this way, Bushey. They are a poor family. Now they'll have two more onions to eat." And so I committed seven more sins that morning.'

I'd gone out to photograph a goat and instead I'd been to Ethiopia and back – and that was before lunch. At lunch it was the turn of the Nazis. We'd gone two coves down the coast to another Bally, largely occupied by Ken Thompson and his family. Ken is a fine sculptor, his large figures are outside and inside Irish Catholic cathedrals, and his delicate illustrations and italic writing are chiselled into tombstones, most notably on the Memorial to Innocent Victims beside Westminster Abbey's Great West Door. Ken is a dynamic man, passionate about whatever he is currently involved with. Over lunch it is about a book he has just read – Christabel Bielenberg's *The Past is Myself*, her best-selling memoir about her wartime life married to a German in Nazi Germany. Ken tells us how fascinating and uplifting the story is. One of the guests, Sally Phipps, mentions that after the war the Bielenbergs came to live in County Carlow, not far from where she and her mother used to live.

Sally Phipps turns out to be the daughter of the Anglo-Irish playwright and novelist, Molly Keane, renowned for her acerbic writing and sharp tongue. Sally is writing her biography. Later she tells me she didn't want to upset our host's enthusiasm by saying that her mother wasn't too impressed by Christabel Bielenberg's writing. 'In fact I've just been reading one of my mother's last reviews for the *Spectator*. It was about Bielenberg's book. Her opening sentence was "Christabel Bielenberg could domesticate even a public hanging." It's about now, as lunchtime effortlessly merges into teatime, that I begin to feel that everything is splendidly connected, that these Ballys are not the back of beyond at all, but the centre of it, maybe even the front of it.

The Cloyne Report on child abuse by the Bishop and some of the diocesan clergy and the subsequent Vatican cover-up has just come out. Cloyne is just up the road, but nobody mentions the subject. Conversationally this is clearly a no-go area at an ecumenical lunch party like this – religious beliefs and opinions must be left on the doorstep with the wet umbrellas. However, I did think it only polite to enquire about the economy. I received brief replies varying from 'just desperate' to 'totally banjaxed'. 'At least you're better off than the Greeks,' I ventured. 'Yes,' Ken said, 'but they've got the sun.'

That all happened in the first thirty-six hours. We still had ten days to go. Fortunately we know from experience that it's important, whatever Bally you're in, to mark clearly in your diary a day or two devoted to silence – other people's silence.

Up and Away

I did not have a good war, education-wise. I was ferried back and forth across the Irish Sea between my Russian-Jewish-Irish grandparents, all four of them, and my parents in London, where my father was a GP in much-bombed Hackney. I had logged up eight schools before I ended up at the Perse School in Cambridge. I took to wandering round the colleges, and realised that I was living in an extraordinarily beautiful town. I also became aware of undergraduates. They appeared to be only a year or two older than me and, blessedly, of both sexes. If anyone was having a better time than me in Cambridge, they were. My decision was easily made. I was only good at one subject – history. I would read it at Cambridge, if they'd have me.

There were only two hurdles – passing the entrance exams and, if I did, convincing my parents to let me go there. The former proved somewhat easier than the latter. Gonville and Caius College gave me a place to read History after I had completed National Service. I went home to tackle my parents. Superficially, they were impressed, particularly as I'd been offered a place by two colleges. I explained that Gonville and Caius was only one college, rather like

Fortnum and Mason's was only one shop. I could see that my success made them deeply uneasy. Clever children, they believed, went to a university to become doctors or lawyers. No one in the family had ever been to a university to study an arts subject. Nor, at that time, had any of their friends' children. They knew that they should feel proud, but instead they felt threatened.

To them the very idea of Cambridge embodied the upper-class British ethos that my father found most inimical and intimidating, the world of Lady Sweedlepipe and Lord Vogenshmeer, the imaginary characters he had invented as a convenient shorthand for it. All his old Irish-Jewish prejudices reasserted themselves. Not only might I abandon whatever was left of my Jewish identity, but I would trade it in for a mess of Establishment pottage, a mixture of bacon and seafood, snobbery and seductive Gentile women. If I would take his advice and read medicine at Trinity College, Dublin, I might graduate into someone he could still recognise. There would be family and friends there to keep an eye on me. He had heard and believed stories about Oxford and Cambridge being places where young people went 'off the rails'.

First- and second-generation Jewish parents have traditionally been obsessed with the professions. Such jobs confer security and status in a society that is still not entirely to be trusted. My parents had no idea what one did with History afterwards. 'Afterwards' became some mystical eternity in which you had to do something with History. I hadn't a much better idea than my parents about what I would do 'afterwards'. Maybe I could teach, or even write, but more immediately I just wanted to spend three years of my life at Cambridge reading History.

Five years before, I had locked myself in a bathroom in Ireland to avoid going back to England. Now I desperately wanted to stay in England and had to think of a reverse strategy. Edwin Keppel Bennett suddenly sprang to mind. Known to everyone at Caius as Francis Bennett, he was the senior tutor who had interviewed me when I took the scholarship exam. He was about sixty, silver-haired, very dapper in black jacket, waistcoat and striped trousers, the quintessence of an old school Cambridge don. Even better for my purposes was his wonderfully kind, avuncular manner. If he could put me at my ease in such an interview, he might just do the same for my parents. I suggested that they go and see Mr Bennett and ask him what you did with History 'afterwards'. Amazingly, for once my father was not *shemadik*, and they agreed.

Shemadik is an extremely rare Yiddish word, best defined as a condition that occurs when excessive modesty combines with social embarrassment. It most frequently hit my father when forced to confront what he considered Establishment authority, either Gentile or Jewish. In such a situation he could cope only if he was fired by anger as a result of injustice. His periodic attacks of *shemadik* irritated my mother, whose reaction was always to say she would confront whatever it was on her own. So, to compensate for what she saw as my father's cowardice, she went in all guns blazing. Invariably the result was disastrous.

My father knew they would get lost in Cambridge, so he insisted that I go with them and drive. He had an *idée fixe* that East Anglia was perpetually shrouded in either fog or mist, and if he had to drive through either he would get a migraine. When we arrived, fog-free, in Cambridge I showed them the coffee shop we should meet in after their appointment, and went with them as far as the first court of Caius College and pointed them towards Mr Bennett's rooms. As I watched them walk across the courtyard our roles suddenly seemed reversed. I was the anxious parent, they the children, small and vulnerable, going into the unknown. I spent the next half-hour walking abstractedly on the Backs, oblivious of their beauty.

They came into the coffee shop, and I knew everything was all right just from the look of them. Then my father bestowed his highest accolade on Francis Bennett: 'What a gentleman!'

They had all had a nice chat. My mother was glowing with the experience of meeting Mr Bennett and how well they had all got on. 'Your father, of course, was too *shemadik* to ask him.' Then she added with pride, 'I had to.' 'What?' I asked with dread. 'I asked him what you could do with History afterwards.' 'What did he say?' 'He said,' she imitated his surprised upper-class tone, 'What can he do with History afterwards? Mrs Price, your son will be an educated man.'

Perhaps that was not the most insightful, mind-expanding answer to the question, but there was clearly some alchemy about that moment, about the man who said it, the way he said it, and where it was said – he had the most beautiful rooms in the college. Whatever it was, he managed to calm their fears, and offer their son a future, some small share of the 'afterwards'. Maybe they realised that Mr Bennett, his college and becoming 'an educated man' were experiences they should not deprive me of. Or maybe it was just that they were from 'dirty old Dublin' and their parents were from '*der heim*' and, with his full head of silver hair in that seductive setting, Mr Bennett held all the cards.

If you can walk on air, you must presumably be able to drive on it. That was how I drove them home. There was no fog or mist, no migraine, no mention of *shemadik* again, but my parents were strangely quiet. Maybe they had a premonition that everything they feared most was about to come to pass.

An Irish Weekend in Wales

I last played rugby at college, but, after a very minor injury, took early retirement. I have remained a fan, watching mostly from an armchair when there's a big game on telly – with fruit at half-time. Twickenham is not that far away, but I'd never been to an international match. The crowds and the cost kept me away, so when tickets for this year's World Cup went on sale, I didn't bother to apply. Then one day I had a phone call from my brother, who had just had a seventy-fifth birthday. As a present, his two daughters, with great resourcefulness, had got him two tickets for a World Cup match. How did I feel about a weekend in Cardiff – good seats behind the goalposts – to see Ireland play France? A nano-second ... and I said 'Yes!' It would be one of the key matches and, because of our parentage and early upbringing, we were ardent Ireland supporters.

Now the brother (to use an Irish-ism) knows the ropes at big events. He had everything planned – the time of the train, seats reserved, the hotel booked, route to the Millennium Stadium marked on his map, and his green bobble-hat packed. It was my first time in Cardiff, but judging by the colour of their hats and flags, most of the people on the street were either French or Irish. In fact, the only Welshman we met on our whole trip was our black taxi-driver. When he heard we were supporting Ireland, he confided that he didn't much like the French – 'Not very friendly, and think they know everything.'

We checked into the Hotel Mercure, part of a French chain, and guessed the Irish might be in a minority here. We were right. Next morning at breakfast, I wore my shamrock green shirt, a normal button-down with nothing written on it. At the buffet we were surrounded by men in electric blue shirts with Allez France! emblazoned on them. They smiled and said bonjour, full of EU bonhomie. On the way to the ground there was a sea of green with small islands of blue in it, and occasional bursts of 'Alouette'. Waiting to cross at a crowded zebra were six men and women, each with a big individual letter on their shirts spelling F-R-A-N-C-E. Ingenious, but impractical – when they made it to the other side they were C-A-N-E-R-F. When we reached the mighty walls of Cardiff Castle it looked as if it were being besieged by a huge foreign army. By now, the brother was wearing his green bobble-hat. I felt a surge of tribalism coming on, and bought a small Irish tricolour at a stall that did face-painting. A young woman was having a shamrock done on each cheek and a harp on her forehead – at £5 an item.

If you've watched most of your rugby on television, the first sight of a vast crowded stadium is overwhelming – the pitch so big, the grass so green, the officials inspecting the turf so real, everything so three-dimensional. When the teams came out the roar of the crowd was deafening.

Judging by the noise, we were in the Irish section, except that in front of us there were six men who were dressed as, or maybe really were, Breton onion-sellers. They were all in berets and horizontally striped vests with identical false blade moustaches and strings of onions around their necks. The chatty man on my right was wearing an elaborate leprechaun hat. He was proud to tell me the star Irish fly-half lived next door to him. The 'Marseillaise' and 'Ireland's Call' were sung by the two teams and 72,000 spectators – goose-pimple time. The whistle went, the volume of sound went up and down according to who had the ball. Our seats were on the end of the row. Their only drawback was the number of times we had to stand up to let someone out to fetch more beer. Then, of course, they had to come back. Later, they'd be back again, the call of the bladder stronger than Ireland's. Just before half-time Ireland had a slender lead and then tragedy struck. Three of their star players were injured and had to be stretchered off. One of them was my leprechaun friend's neighbour. He clapped his hands to his head and said, 'Ah sure now we're finished!'

In the huge queues for the bars and toilets, the Irish were unusually subdued, but after half-time, everything changed. Whatever their coach had said to them in the dressing-room, it worked. The Irish, with their replacements, outplayed the French, who did not score again. The Breton onion-sellers had gone quiet. At every Irish score the crowd were on their feet, arms aloft, cheering, the brother among them. I waved my flag. At each score, my leprechaun friend threw his arm round my shoulder and shouted 'Unbelievable!' It was – Ireland won 24-9.

Back in the hotel bar, the brother ordered draught Guinness. The French started drifting in. I was still wearing my green shirt. They were polite to us, but the bonhomie was *un peu moins évidente*. On the train back to Paddington, we agreed that there couldn't have been a better birthday present – but if the Irish hadn't won...

Sic Transit Gloria

Usually, somewhere in the world, *Sunset Boulevard*, the musical, is playing with a big star in the lead. In April, it returns to London, with Glenn Close. By opening for a limited season at the Coliseum, home of English National Opera, Andrew Lloyd Webber's musical, worthy or not, acquires opera status. But for me, there will only ever be one *Sunset Boulevard* and it's a film, Billy Wilder's, and only one star: Gloria Swanson.

In 1950 Hollywood thought it very brave of Swanson, coaxed out of retirement, to play Norma Desmond, the ageing silent film star. She lives in faded splendour with her butler, Max, who was once her director. He is played by Erich von Stroheim, a masterstroke of casting, as he had, in real life, been Swanson's director, and they had fought constantly. Norma is planning her great movie comeback. When William Holden, as a young screenwriter, first sees her, he says, 'Hey! You're Norma Desmond. You used to be in silent pictures. You used to be big.' Swanson pulls herself up to her full 5ft 2in, and with a disdainful glare says, 'I am big. It's the pictures that got small.' And she plays Norma Desmond 'big' from opening shot to final fade, a perfect example of her line: 'We didn't need dialogue. We had faces.'

I first saw the film when I was working in New York. It was fourteen years old, and already a classic. I was mesmerised by Swanson's performance and, a few days later, had one of those coincidences that produce an odd tingle. I was visiting friends at Croton-on-Hudson, about forty miles upriver from New York, and we were on a country walk. My host pointed out a small French-style château. That, I was told, had been Gloria Swanson's and Joe Kennedy's love nest. He had given her the house as a present.

My knowledgeable host told me about the millionaire Kennedy's foray into Hollywood in the late 1920s. He invested profitably in several studios, and had even toyed with the idea of starting one himself, but he didn't like the people with whom he had to do business. Most of them were Jewish, and he called them 'pants-pressers'. If it hadn't been for them, there might have been a Kennedy Studios, and his three good-looking sons would have been movie stars not politicians.

He came back East having acquired several more millions and Gloria Swanson as a mistress. Their affair lasted three years, despite Kennedy having a wife and nine children in Boston. Swanson's ex-lover became ambassador to Britain in 1938, and spent two years advising Roosevelt that Britain could not win the war and that the US could and should do business with Hitler. Swanson herself gave up making films, but acted on Broadway and on television, and ran her own lingerie business.

Cut to 1980 – the annual American Film Festival was

taking place at Deauville, and an American magazine asked me to cover it. The guest of honour was Gloria Swanson, and they were going to show *Queen Kelly*, her last silent film. Financed and produced by Joe Kennedy, it was directed by Erich von Stroheim, until he was fired for making it too outrageous. Swanson then directed a changed ending herself. If I went, I could see *Sunset Boulevard* again. I might even see Swanson, and how she had weathered thirty years after being Norma Desmond.

Sunset Boulevard stood the test of time, but *Queen Kelly* was a melodramatic mishmash: beautiful convent student abducted by lecherous prince, fate worse than death, abused by mad, sadistic queen, and then the changed ending – suicide, with contrite prince visiting her tomb. Throughout, the star was doing amazing face-acting.

When I interviewed her, however, Swanson was not in the least melodramatic. In her hotel suite, she poured herb tea for me and an elegant man in his fifties, who was introduced simply as Douglas. An ex-husband? Her Press agent? A chaperone? As she handed me the aromatic cup of tea, she explained that she had always been very missionary about health food and drink. She was a marvellous advertisement for its benefits, especially for someone who had had six husbands and Joe Kennedy.

She sat very straight-backed, in an elegant black dress, some discreet jewellery, hair and make-up impeccable, as befitted the star of *Sunset Boulevard*, whose last line had been 'All right, Mr DeMille, I'm ready for my close-up.'

After fifty-five years, Gloria Swanson was not taking *Queen Kelly* too seriously. I asked her if she could remember the original ending. 'Yes. I ended up running a brothel in German East Africa.' She gave an expressive shrug.

After her numerous fallings out with von Stroheim as a director, how had it been ordering him about as her butler in *Sunset Boulevard*?

'Fun,' she said with edge. 'Anyway, you were terrific,' I said. 'Thank you.' At eighty-one, her smile was still very seductive.

As I was leaving, she turned to the so-far silent man, 'Douglas, look at his ear lobes.' My hands went to my ears. 'What's wrong with them?' 'They're very large. Just like mine.' She gestured at hers. They were very large too.

'It's a sign of longevity,' she said. 'Great!' was all I could think to say.

Gloria Swanson died four years later. As for me – well, so far so good.

Spare Me the Organ Recital

In a recent interview Ian McKellen, an energetic 72-year-old, admitted that he didn't much enjoy mixing with fellow-thesps of his own age. They talked too much about illness, their own and other people's, about who was still with us, who wasn't, and who was about to move from the first category into the second.

I don't mix much with actors myself but I know what he means. I can't remember exactly at what age this 'intimations of mortality' talk began – at a guess in one's early sixties. Anyway, it seems to affect retirees and non-retirees equally. You phone up some of them, ask how they are and they tell you – at length. This type of conversation has become known as the 'Organ Recital', a phrase attributed to the septuagenarian novelist Philip Roth.

I have a friend who copes with this by saying brusquely: 'We'll do three minutes on health and that's it.' I don't imagine he's now phoned much by his friends. But I generalise. There are some stoics: when asked how they are they say 'Fine'. It's up to you to judge whether the word is said with confidence, defensively, or after a slight pause. Later you may learn from their partner that 'fine' was a slight exaggeration, sadly sometimes a fatal one.

The most interesting aspect of the Organ Recital is the one that occurs on meeting old friends seen irregularly. It's impossible not to register that they've joined the obese brigade, or lost most of their hair, or keep asking you to repeat what you're saying. There's no denying the competitive edge to these meetings. Everyone longs to be told, with genuine admiration, that they don't look their age. But don't trust anyone who says you look only half your age. They're after something.

I meet my oldest friend, Wally (not his real name of course) for lunch at reasonably regular intervals. To some extent we have aged together, so any changes in appearance and health have been gradual and not too shocking. The exception was the time when he shaved off his thinning hair to be à la mode, probably a professional requirement, as he is very successful in a business that puts great store by appearances.

We first met at primary school, but after that we were not often in the same place at the same time. Occasionally we overlapped somewhere, most memorably during National Service for a brief period at an Army training camp. One morning our company was being drilled by a Guards sergeant-major. In his best stentorian voice he roared at us to 'Right Dress', the drill to get us perfectly in line. Dutifully we jerked our heads to the right, shot our right arms out to our neighbours' shoulders and shuffled our feet quickly to bring us into line, then snapped back to attention.

The sergeant-major pointed his pace stick at a man in the front rank. It was my friend Wally. He screamed at him with the obscene poetry of his ilk: 'YOU! IF YOU'RE RIGHT DRESSED MY COCK'S A KIPPER.' He then marched smartly to the end of the front line and looked down it. With extraordinary honesty he roared: 'GOOD GOD MY COCK'S A KIPPER!' We painfully suppressed our laughter, as laughing on parade was a criminal offence. What we really wanted to do was applaud.

We had other fairly seminal experiences together and, as with so many friendships, laughter has been its cement. We don't laugh about the ageing process, but we get it out of the way before the first course arrives. As far as we can tell we're not doing badly. Unlike many of our contemporaries, we still have both our original hips. He grudgingly admits he's now on two hearing aids. I confess that I'm still only on one. I like him. I don't want to score points. We are both grateful to be still working – and for ourselves. We move onto the healthy, familiar ground of recent scandals among family and friends and the depressing state of contemporary politics and culture.

On health grounds we decline dessert. With coffee I remember to ask him how he and his wife are settling into their new London flat.

'It's too small.'

'Didn't you notice that before you bought it?' 'Well ... we just thought of it being a ... you know, a ... what's that word ... you know, a ... in London. What's the damn word?'

He was clearly getting distressed about the vocabulary

breakdown. I remembered he had a house near Henley and his missing word came to me. 'You mean a pied-à-terre.'

'No, I know the French word. It's the bloody English word I've forgotten. What the hell is it? This is happening to me more and more – forgetting names and things. Does this happen to you?'

God, we were going to end up on the ageing process after all. I acted the wise, loyal old friend who would be there when he finally went gaga. 'Of course. Often. Happens to everyone. It's not Alzheimer's. Just relax. Put it out of your mind for five minutes and it'll come.'

'How the hell do I put it out of my mind?'

'Willpower.'

He ignored my advice. 'I've nearly got it. Two words – like pot ... pot-something.'

'Potpourri, pot roast...' I suggested. My facetiousness didn't amuse him. 'Two words. Begins with a d ... ddddd ... or maybe a p ... ppp... Something like post ... poste restante.' I couldn't resist. 'You live in a poste restante in north London and it's too small for you?'

'Very funny. I'm damn well going to get it.'

Now I knew why Wally had been so successful. He had determination: never give up – get there in the end.

'Wait, wait. It's b ... bbb ... two small words.'

I got there first. Bolthole. A bolthole in London.

'That's it. Bolthole.' He was hugely relieved. 'Thank you.'

'A pleasure. Any time you're stuck just ring me on my mobile.'

'I haven't got your mobile number.' 'I'll give it to you.' He got out a pen and address book. 'It's 0778 ... er ... 344 ...

no ... 67 ... no, wait ... 07734 ... I can never remember it. Too bloody long.'

'Just relax. Put it out of your mind. Phone me when you remember it.' He smiled. The score: one all.

DEADLY ESTATES

The coincidences began as soon as our offer for the house in Muswell Hill was accepted. I was in the middle of filming the pilot episode of a TV series I had written. The next day I realised our leading actress, Liza Goddard, was distinctly under par. In a coffee-break she confided why. She had just been gazumped for a house she and her husband were desperate to buy. It was perfect for them. She was married to the rock'n'roll star Alvin Stardust, and the house had a huge cellar that would make a wonderful recording studio. Where was the house, I asked? In Muswell Hill, she said. What street? Cranley Gardens, she said. What number? I guessed what the answer would be and was right. I had just bought Mr and Mrs Stardust's dream house. I admitted the buyer was me. She looked at me as though I was a deadly snake who had just crawled out from under a rock. I protested that I hadn't gazumped her, I had simply offered the asking price. She looked dubious. She said she had made a good offer and had been accepted. Nobody had told me that, I said. In that case the estate agents and the owners had screwed them, she said. 'Not a unique experience,' I said. Perhaps that wasn't a sympathetic enough response as I felt a slight chill for the rest of the filming.

We moved into the house in early February 1983. It badly needed redecorating and we called in the two Jimmies, middle-aged Irish cousins who were always cheerful and only turned the radio on for the big races. On their fourth day they turned up looking less than cheerful.

'Quite a commotion in the street,' the older Jimmy said.

'What sort of commotion?'

'Police, reporters, TV cameras. Didn't you hear the news last night?'

I shook my head. They looked embarrassed and the younger Jimmy passed me his *Daily Mirror*. The headline announced the arrest of one Dennis Nilsen for murdering a large, but as yet unspecified, number of young men in his flat in Cranley Gardens. You may recall that Nilsen was caught because, after strangling his victims, he dismembered them and put them down the main drain. Neighbours downstream of him – we were fortunately three houses up the hill – complained of blocked drains. Dyno-Rod were called out and got a nasty surprise. The police followed soon after.

The Jimmies were decent men who didn't enjoy being the bringers of bad news. They probably realised we'd paid a fortune for the house and that overnight it had become worth only half-a-fortune. I went out into the street. It was, as reported, a great commotion of police cars with flashing lights, television cameras, reporters and bug-eyed spectators. When I saw Kate Adie in front of our house with a hand-mike I knew we were in real trouble. In those days she only did serious civil wars and major catastrophes and atrocities. Later that week when I looked out of my study window I could see police digging in the wasteland behind our houses. Tourist coaches were now parking outside our house to disembark ghouls with cameras to take their souvenir pictures of the slaughterhouse. A couple of the coaches even came from Italy. Meanwhile, Nilsen was confessing freely and fully and, to our dismay, our street hogged the headlines for weeks. He had killed up to six young men in his eighteen months in his Cranley Gardens flat and probably about nine in his previous flat in Melrose Avenue, Cricklewood. Police forensics were working overtime to establish the exact number.

My wife Judy's and my initial reaction was to want instant out. Our new home had been poisoned for us. We would pay off the Jimmies, sell the house and go and live as far away from Muswell Hill as we could – South America, South London even. But who, I asked, would now buy the house given its grisly locale? Judy had a brainwave – the Alvin Stardusts. If he really wanted that recording studio in the basement desperately enough...

'No one could be that desperate,' I said.

'Just try,' she said. 'We could bring the price down a bit.'

'We might have to give it away.'

But I did phone. Liza answered the phone and was affable. After a few pleasantries I said, 'You've probably heard about what's happened in Cranley Gardens.'

'How could one not?' Did I detect schadenfreude in her voice?

'My wife's been very upset by it all. More sensitive soul than I am, but I was just wondering...'

Liza didn't even wait for her cue. 'The answer's no. No way.' And that really ended the conversation.

A week or so later I went to a Writers' Guild function at the Purcell Room on the South Bank. I found myself talking to Bill Craig, a popular Scots TV-writer, and novelist Fay Weldon. I told them of my recent move to Cranley Gardens. They both went a little pale, but I was getting used to that. Bill Craig interrupted me: 'That's bloody incredible. I live in Cricklewood – Melrose Avenue, where he did the other half-dozen or so. I was probably putting out my garbage bags next to his – with the bits in them.' Fay Weldon now looked even paler. 'Three weeks ago my daughter went to the Job Centre in Kentish Town. That's where he worked. She was interviewed by him.' There was a silence. We couldn't decide what the odds were against a coincidence like that, but we did agree he wouldn't have been caught, or at least not so quickly, if he'd had a car. With a car you can bundle the body into the boot and drive it out to Rickmansworth reservoir or the Lea near Bishop's Stortford – well, we were all writers. Without a car the problem of corpse-disposal is tricky and very messy.

For a while, to avoid morbid questioning, I didn't tell people where I lived. The other residents in the street were equally traumatised. Some petitioned Haringey Council to destroy the house and rename the street, as had happened to Christie's house in Rillington Place. The council turned down the suggestion. Instead some developers bought the house for a knockdown price and refurbished the flats. The estate agent involved advertised them emphasising the Nilsen connection as a selling point. The advertisement was withdrawn after local objections to the Estate Agents' Association. The flats were sold without difficulty, but at under the going rate. Inevitably the couple who bought Nilsen's actual flat were interviewed by the local paper and seemed to like the idea of living in a famous flat. At the Old Bailey, Nilsen, thirty-eight at the time, was found guilty on six counts of murder and two of attempted murder, though he had actually murdered over fifteen.

It took some years for people, especially taxi drivers, to forget that Cranley Gardens had been the home of Britain's record-holding serial killer, but eventually house prices soared in line with everywhere else. My TV pilot was made but never became a series.

We stayed on in our house for another seventeen years before moving somewhere smaller with, so far, no psychopathic neighbours. Nilsen is now in the 24th year of his life sentence. Alvin Stardust still tours his rock'n'roll show, mainly up north where he lives. Liza Goddard lives in Norfolk with another husband. Kate Adie, now mainly on radio, has written her autobiography and doesn't mention Cranley Gardens.

The Funeral was
a Dead Loss

Arthur, my father-in-law, lived alone in a small flat in Notting Hill, surrounded by his collection. It was not a collection of anything in particular, he just hated throwing things away. One had to fight one's way through stacks of back numbers of the *New Statesman* just to get into his living-room.

He was, after having a firmly Christian upbringing, a convinced atheist and socialist. We dreaded the time when we would have to dispose of his collection but, inevitably, that time did come.

There was no mention in his will about the disposal of this collection but, thoughtfully, he left instructions for his own disposal. His time in the Merchant Navy had given him a love of the sea and years later, when he could afford it, he took annual cruises. He must have hoped that he would die on one of them because his will expressed the wish to be buried at sea.

Mr Hoades, the local undertaker, tried to be helpful. He suggested cremation and the scattering of the ashes when we next went to the seaside. We said we weren't planning a seaside holiday. Was I a fisherman, Mr Hoades asked? He had noted that I lived in North London and said Rickmansworth reservoir was a possible place 'for the scattering'.

We settled for an urn in the garden of remembrance at the crematorium. Arthur would have to forgive us. After all, it wasn't our fault that he had died between cruises. We informed Mr Hoades that the deceased was an atheist and had left instructions for a non-denominational funeral. 'No problem there,' he said. 'We normally arrange those with the Humanist Society. They do it nicely.'

It was a small and awkward funeral. My mother-in-law was there, not grieving too deeply as they had been separated and had scarcely seen each other in the previous twenty-five years. My sister-in-law made up the family party. There was a distinct absence of professional colleagues, as Arthur had been an unhappy accountant. His real passions were for pottery and stamps so I assumed that the other dozen or so mourners were probably potters or philatelists. For my wife's and mother-in-law's sake, I was relieved that no mysterious, grieving women in black turned up. Looking back, I would have preferred that to what happened next.

The coffin appeared, followed a few moments later by a priest in full Anglican rig: cassock, chasuble and clutching the Book of Common Prayer. He mounted the pulpit and faced us. My wife gripped my arm. 'What's he doing here?' she hissed.

'He must be at the wrong funeral.'

'We are gathered here together to mourn the passing of Arthur...' Oh God, he wasn't at the wrong funeral. Damn that idiot undertaker.

'Man that is born of woman hath but a short time to live...'

Well, Arthur couldn't take exception to that. I breathed a short-lived sigh of relief before the priest was addressing himself to 'God most holy our holy and merciful saviour.' My wife was gripping my arm again and there were tears in her eyes. 'My mother's upset too. You must stop it.'

'Stop it? How?' I'd heard of people stopping marriages but never funerals. And there was another embarrassing, personal complication for me. I am Jewish, not observant, but definitely not Christian. What was a nice Jewish boy doing stopping a Christian funeral? But how would I feel if somebody mistakenly gave me one? The flat clerical voice had reached 'the sure and certain hope of the Resurrection to eternal life…' I was on my feet and heading for the pulpit. Then, out of the corner of my eye, I saw Hoades the undertaker standing at one side of the chapel. I moved over to him and whispered fiercely, 'What happened to the Humanists? You've got to stop this right away. The family's very upset.'

'Sorry. Terrible mistake,' he said, and headed for the pulpit. To attract the priest's attention he pulled on his chasuble. The priest stopped and Hoades whispered in his ear. There was a puzzled mumbling from the mourners. The priest looked flustered, then turned to us.

'I gather there's been some misunderstanding and the deceased didn't wish a Christian funeral. Obviously I can't unsay what I've said…' He gave us an awkward smile. 'But I'll do my best to finish the service.' His best consisted of continuing to read from the prayer book but simply skipping words every time he came to a mention of Almighty God or Our Lord Jesus Christ.

It was a stumbling, stuttering performance, sentences trailing away incomprehensibly. For a moment he thought he'd be all right with the Lord's Prayer but quickly realised that omitting the Our Father and anything about his kingdom coming, made a nonsense of it all. I had begun to feel sorry for the poor man but then he totally alienated me.

His voice strengthened and he read out, 'I heard a voice from heaven saying unto me, from henceforth blessed are the dead which die in the Lord...' He shut his prayer book, looked at us defiantly, and launched into, as I best remember it, 'Look, it's all very well not having any belief here on earth but afterwards in the after-life, that all Christians believe in, people like Arthur Fenton may finally see there is a God and maybe even come to believe in him.'

What a cheap, chiselling thing to suggest – a post-mortem conversion. I was too angry to speak to him afterwards. We didn't have a lot to say to Hoades either when he apologised profusely.

Afterwards I tried to console my still-very-upset wife by reminding her of her father's wry sense of humour. Maybe, I said, if there was an after-life or some sort of heaven, and her father, good socialist and atheist that he was, was up there somewhere, he would be having a good laugh. If one was able or allowed to laugh there, that is.

'You sound like just like that stupid priest,' she said.

HIGH WIND IN ISFAHAN

You have to change planes in Tehran to get to Isfahan. The latter, I was told, was a beautiful city and I should visit the main mosques if I had the time. It was 1978, a year before the Shah was overthrown, but I didn't know that then and nor did he. The Shah Abbas hotel in Isfahan turned out to be at least five-star. No doubt the odd secret policeman lurked in the foyer – after all it was a very repressive regime – but surely a film-script doctor hadn't too much to fear from them. Though I had heard there was government money in the film.

In those days, film rewrites were the gilt/guilt on the professional writer's gingerbread, a lucrative and sometimes stimulating break from lonely vigils with one's current opus. This particular doctoring job, however, was not the standard chore. The sick screenplay arrived at very short notice with numerous coloured pages indicating scenes already shot. I'd never before worked on a film actually in production. As re-shooting scenes would be prohibitively expensive, the freedom to rewrite would be strictly limited and had to be done on location.

The script was based on *Caravans*, a novel by James

Michener, the best-selling American novelist who special-
ised in melodramatic sagas covering vast swathes of history
set in exotic cultures.

The basic plot concerned a young American woman who
marries an Afghan student, goes home with him, turns
native and disappears. An American consul looks for her
among an assortment of native goodies and baddies, one
of whom is Zulfiqar, a Baluchi warlord, played by the film's
star – Anthony Quinn.

On my first night in Isfahan, the producer, Elmo Williams,
took me to dinner, appropriately in an Afghan restaurant.
He was a quietly-spoken American in his early sixties. Over
the starters he admitted he hadn't thought about retirement
till he'd started making this movie. His young director, who
had directed a very successful Western, wasn't doing so well
with a Middle Eastern. He didn't get on with the cast and
they didn't get on with each other. It was debilitatingly
hot shooting in the desert, and his two young American
stars, Jennifer O'Neill and Michael Sarrazin, vied with each
other for who could go down sick most often, and have a
consultant flown in from Harley Street.

We'd finished the dessert before Elmo got to Anthony
Quinn. He and Elmo were the same age, which was apparently all they had in common. Quinn was of Irish-Mexican
extraction, a sometime boxing champion and, according to
Elmo, not the easiest of men at the best of times – which
these weren't. Quinn wanted the script rewritten to give
Zulfiqar a proper dramatic climax.

'Couldn't he have said that when he first read the script?'
'He was too busy negotiating his fee. Actors!' Elmo

sighed, and told me how he'd once worked on a couple of Disney movies. 'It was great. You got fed up with your stars, you just tore them up.'

Elmo introduced me to Quinn early next morning. He was pushing his racing bike through the courtyard of the hotel. Apparently he cycled ten miles every morning before shooting. He looked every inch a very fit, sixty-year-old, ex-boxing champion. I'd probably seen him in a dozen films, but remembered him best as the life-affirming peasant guru in *Zorba the Greek*.

'So you're the genius who's going to pull this piece together?' he said.

'That's right,' I said. It was too early to come up with a better line.

Elmo and I had our script conference on the hour's drive out to the desert location. He liked what I'd thought up on the flight out, and warned me that the four competing stars would all bang my ear. I should smile but not listen too carefully. He advised a special smile for Behrouz Vossoughi, a big Iranian star who was close to the royal family. Elmo lowered his voice so the Iranian driver wouldn't hear – 'especially Princess Ashraf, the Shah's twin sister.'

In the desert it was too hot to smile while the actors, in turn, banged my ear. Behrouz Vossoughi banged it least. He was a handsome and extremely courteous man of around thirty. Later he introduced me to the best Beluga caviar and never once demanded a rewrite in exchange.

The bulk of the writing had to be done in two weeks so I didn't move far from my large desk. From it I could look across an inner courtyard to the suite opposite. One morning I saw a man in uniform standing motionless on the parapet above the suite holding a sub-machine gun. He was watching me working. Was this how they treated their script-doctors? If you'd said two weeks they made sure it was two weeks? In a panic I raced down to reception. 'There's a man with a machine gun...' The receptionist nodded. Farah Diba, the Shah's wife, was staying at the hotel for a few days. It was one of her bodyguards. 'You won't get shot if you stay in your room,' the receptionist smiled. Iranians have a great sense of humour.

Farah Diba moved on, and apart from the caviar and a couple of mosques there were few distractions, so I finished on time. I had written a dramatic denouement for Zulfiqar: he dies saving the strayed American maiden. Elmo and the director seemed happy with what I'd done and we met up with the cast in Elmo's hotel suite to discuss the changes.

First, some dilatory chat and then suddenly Quinn was advancing on me, clutching the new script, face contorted with anger. I was sitting on a low sofa and he leaned over me. He spat out, 'You think this is an ending for me? To die? I never die in my films.' He thumped his fist down on the sofa by my right ear. He pulled his fist back again. I struggled to get up. If I was going to be punched by an ex-champ I would take it like a man – standing up.

Instead he waved the script in my face and launched into a diatribe that memory synopsises into 'I don't die ... I'm Zorba... Zorba the Greek... I stand for the life-force ... I influenced a generation of our boys in Vietnam ... together we ended the war ... we chose life ... I don't die in movies – not for you, not for fucking anybody.' He hurled the script on the floor and stormed out. It was as good as anything he'd done since *Lawrence of Arabia*.

After a brief cooling-off period Elmo went to beard the life-force in his suite. Next morning Elmo, now looking in his late rather than early sixties, told me Quinn was adamant about not dying. They would continue shooting my rewritten scenes but, to satisfy Quinn, find a new writer for the ending. Elmo asked me if I knew an experienced screenwriter who might fly out straight away for the same money as me? Yes, I did. My friend Michael fitted the bill and had just started paying a horrendous amount of alimony.

Michael flew in and reprieved Zulfiqar so he could ride off into the sunset. The film was finished on budget if not schedule. The reviews were not exactly glowing but, happily, neither my name nor Michael's appeared on the credits. According to the *Time Out* Film Guide: 'Unfortunately, this slice of epic schlock has all the seductive power of a syphilitic camel. There is some atmospheric photography, but Zorba the Arab inevitably spoils it all with ethnic dancing of appalling jollity. No great sheiks.'

However, the film did get one Oscar nomination – for best costume design – and Michael sent me a case of good claret.

SCAMS I HAVE KNOWN

There is something very special about those brown envelopes which contain a Penalty Notice. They exude an unpleasant odour of 'you have been caught', and they usually come as a complete surprise. This particular brown job was from Transport for London – a Penalty Notice for driving in the congestion zone without paying the fee. There were supporting colour photographs, unmistakably of my dark blue VW Golf with my number-plate driving in the congestion zone at Pentonville Road, NW1, at 5.47 pm on 3rd October 2008.

My first reaction was 'couldn't be'. I vaguely knew the location, but it wasn't a route I would ever take. I raced to my diary. The only entry for that date was an evening film nowhere near NW1. I simply couldn't have been there. Then the doubts of age set in: was this the first warning sign of that illness with the 'A' name I'd rather forget? My wife – could it have been her? No, she said, she'd never driven on the Pentonville Road in her life. Maybe, after all, I had gone into town that day, and came back that way because of some diversion. Perhaps I should go and look at the exact location. It might bring it back to me. I'd have to

go in the evening to avoid the congestion charge. I wasn't
going to let Transport for London drive me to dementia. I
would appeal.

But how do you prove you weren't somewhere? I didn't
have an alibi for myself or my car. The fine was £60. After
fourteen days it rose to £120. To be on the safe side I sent
a cheque for £60 with my appeal. Three weeks later I was
informed that my appeal had been rejected. It was my word
against Transport for London's cameras, and the cameras
had won.

A week later there was another brown envelope on the
doormat. This time it was from Islington Borough Council
– a Penalty Notice for a parking offence at Macdonald
Road, N19, with accompanying photographs of a parked
dark blue Golf with my number-plates. This time my car
and I had an alibi. We had kept a hospital appointment
far from there, and I could prove it. I phoned the police.
They said I had to report the matter and take any documentation to my nearest police station. If I was making an
appeal I would need a Crime Report Number. There was a
long wait before I saw the overworked policewoman on the
desk. She looked at my two penalty notices and said very
matter-of-factly, 'Your plates have been cloned. Happens a
lot these days.'

'Cloned?' I knew it happened to sheep, maybe soon to us,
but not to number-plates.

'How? Why?'

'They have a car, popular make and colour, probably
stolen, and they go round till they find another car just like
it. Not too difficult. Then they write down the registration

number and give it to someone they know who makes duplicate number-plates.'

'And they drive around ignoring meters and congestion charges and I pay their fines?'

'Right. They can also go into service stations, fill up and just drive away. The attendant takes down your number. Or they could do a robbery.'

She took down my particulars and I got my Crime Report Number. 'Now you'll need a password.'

'What for?'

'So you don't go to prison for them.' She had a nice smile when she showed it. 'You could be stopped by the police. They'll be looking for your number.'

For the next few days I drove around nervously waiting for the siren and the flashing lights warning me to pull over. It never happened, but a couple of friendly neighbourhood policemen did turn up on my doorstep. They wanted to know if I'd appealed, and looked at my penalty notices. One of the PCs was particularly interested because he'd had the same thing happen to him a few months before. As they left they had a look at my car. The PC whose car had been cloned had an extraordinary visual memory. He asked to see the Transport for London photos again, and pointed to the number plate on the back of the dark blue Golf in the photo.

'Look. It's got that little blue EU marking that has GB on it.'

He was right. It was tiny on the photo, barely visible, and I'd missed it. He then pointed to the number-plates on my car – no blue EU marking.

'Careless, weren't they?' he said. 'Proves your case, though.'

I re-appealed and had my £60 returned. A month later I had a phone call from a detective constable on the Flying Squad. He told me that two men had been apprehended after a major burglary in Kent. They had been driving a dark blue Golf with the same number-plates as mine. Would I be willing to sign a statement that I didn't know the two men, that it wasn't my car, as previously reported to the police, and provide the necessary documentation, photographs etc? I said I would be very happy to. Their case comes to court next month. My evidence will be there but I won't. My Flying Squad detective said he'll let me know the outcome. I imagine they'll go to prison. I'll be interested to know for how long. At least they'll be going there in their own right and not under my registration number.

THE FIVER SCAM

Locations are important to this story, so let me say that I'm an East Finchley man who rarely ventures into the urban sprawl of Finchley Central. I only went that day because of a shop there that sold swimming earplugs. I arrived to discover that since my last visit it had closed down. I then went to the cash machine of the local NatWest.

The cash machine was beside the entrance. It had a small, waist-high buttress to one side. I put in my card and pin number and keyed in £150. I was suddenly aware of two men standing close behind me. One of them said, in a heavy foreign accent, 'Is that your five pound note?' I looked round and saw a man in his mid-twenties pointing at a five-pound note on the ground beside me. The man with him, and directly behind me, was older and of the same ethnic group. They weren't exactly Mediterranean, somewhere north-east of there. Anyway I didn't see how a five-pound note could have dropped out of my pocket like that.

'I don't think it's mine,' I said.

'Must be mine then,' he said.

Why say it's mine then? Too late I realised it was a trick.

The man had already stooped down, grabbed the five-pound note and taken off up the High Road after his older colleague.

I realised that, being distracted, I hadn't taken my £150 from the slot. I looked back and of course it wasn't there. The older man had obviously taken it. I sprinted after them, shouting. My rational side must have said it was highly dangerous to chase after two men whose combined ages were less than mine, but I was outraged. Would I have been so outraged for £20 or even £50? And what would I do if I caught them?

I wasn't thinking that far ahead. And I did catch the younger one. I grabbed his arm and shouted that I wanted my money back. While the older man kept running, the younger one stayed to argue. He hadn't taken my money. Incredibly, he didn't thump, knife or shoot me. He showed me an empty wallet and allowed me to drag him back to the bank, insisting all the time he hadn't taken my money. 'No, because your bloody friend took it.'

Back in the bank the deputy manager – banks don't seem to have actual managers any more – came out to investigate the noise. My captive kept shouting he hadn't taken any money and flourishing his empty wallet. I kept shouting, 'His accomplice took it.' The deputy told his deputy to call the police. When he heard the P-word, my man and his wallet took off. We chased him out into the street, but he already had a good head start.

Five minutes later a Panda car turned up and I was in the deputy manager's office with two very efficient policemen. PC 1 took down my statement while PC 2 was already on his radio-phone. The only problem I had was describing my robbers.

'Very light brownish...'

'Their ethnic group?'

'Turks, Kurds, Azeris, something like that...' He seemed to get the idea. Later, after I'd signed various forms, he said, sympathetically, 'Afraid you fell for the old fiver scam.' Apparently it was in widespread use among the criminal classes. PC 2's phone rang. He came off the line jubilant. 'We've got the buggers.'

It can't have been more than twenty-five minutes between the police arriving and the two 'buggers' being caught. Based on the information that PC 2 fed his mobile colleagues, they had obviously surmised that the two men had headed for the nearest tube station, Finchley Central, and most likely would get off at the next stop. But which one? Northbound or southbound? Maybe a police car had gone to both. Anyway, two men answering my description had been stopped coming out of my very own and favourite station where the Northern Line, going northwards, emerges into the blessed daylight of East Finchley.

I was away for a week and when I returned there was a message for me to call the NatWest in Finchley Central. The deputy manager informed me that if I checked my recent bank statement, as he had, I would see that on the day of the robbery there was no withdrawal for £150. I was appalled. Was he saying I had made it all up? No, there was a simpler, technical explanation. If the money ordered from the ATM wasn't actually taken within fifteen seconds it was automatically pulled back into the till. Suddenly it all became visually clear – the layout of the ATM, the buttress to one side and the older man beside it. I hadn't leaned over low or far enough to allow him to grab the money. That was why my 'robber' had allowed himself to be dragged back into the bank flourishing his empty wallet. He genuinely didn't have my money. It was an attempted, not a real robbery.

The two men were never charged and I never found out what happened to them. I like to think that, discouraged by our sprightly senior citizens and super-fast policemen, they went home, wherever that is, to rob their own.

THE PHONE SCAM

One Friday I was waiting for a call from a hospital about an appointment – not a matter of life and death, but nonetheless angst-making. A call was also due from my agent about a missing cheque and a favourite cousin coming from the States was going to phone from Heathrow when she landed. Health, wealth and family – a pretty big day for incoming calls.

By 4.30 pm I hadn't had any of these calls and with the weekend coming up I was experiencing mild anxiety. When the phone finally rang it wasn't a call I expected. It was the BT accounts department. Fortunately it wasn't from a Bangalore call-centre or darkest, gibberish Aberdeen. The man had a northern accent and I could actually understand what he said. He wanted to talk about my account. Payment was currently overdue and I had not responded to the recent reminder. That, I said, was impossible. I paid quarterly by direct debit and had never received a reminder. I asked him to hang on while I pulled the relevant folder out of my filing drawer and found the last account. Like all BT bills it was hugely complicated, hard enough to follow when one was feeling calm. I wasn't feeling that calm and I wanted

BT accounts off the phone so I could receive my important calls.

The basic message of my bill seemed clear. My direct debit had been paid but a small amount still owing would appear on my next bill. I told the BT man this. He was polite but firm. I had not responded to their ten-day warning about being disconnected if I did not pay. Disconnected? That was ridiculous. It had to be the bank's mistake. I would talk to them on Monday morning and make them check the payment. That didn't satisfy him. I asked him where he was calling from. 'The Manchester accounts office,' he said. My voice was getting loud and angry enough to bring my wife, Judy, in to see what was wrong. I covered the mouthpiece. 'It's BT. They say we haven't paid the bill. The bastards want to disconnect us.'

I suddenly realised that none of my expected callers would have my mobile phone number. 'You can't disconnect me. I'm expecting some urgent calls.' He suggested that I paid on my debit card now and sorted it out with my bank on Monday. I felt I had no alternative and reached for my card. Judy clearly didn't like this idea. She gestured at the bill, 'Wait a minute,' she said. 'It says you've paid.' I thought of health, wealth and family. What the hell else can I do? I gave the man my debit card number. 'Right,' he said, 'I'll sort that out right away.' And the line went dead.

I tapped on the rest. No sound. Either he hadn't hung up or he'd disconnected me. 'I knew you shouldn't have done that,' Judy said helpfully. Now it was really panic-time for me, but Judy stayed calm, got her mobile phone and called BT. After a lot of dialling of different numbers she eventually got through to someone in accounts and thrust the phone at me. I explained what had happened.

'I'm getting your account up,' the BT woman said. After a few moments she said, 'The account's been paid. Anyway we don't have an accounts office in Manchester. I'm afraid you've been conned. It's happening quite a lot these days.'

'So what do I do now? They've knocked my phone out.'

I must admit that when I finally got through to the right person, BT was not inefficient. The first thing I was told to do was contact my bank on the mobile and ask for the fraud office. There was more complicated dialling, but the bank was clearly geared for this sort of emergency. I gave them my details and was told that within five minutes my debit card would be out of commission. My con-men would have to move quick. I did more dialling and choosing of numbers and then I was back with a sympathetic BT engineer. His advice was straightforward: if someone doesn't hang up their phone you have to unplug all your phones and leave them disconnected for ten minutes. It worked. After ten minutes we were in touch with the outside world again.

Of course there were no messages. When I called the consultant's secretary she had gone home for the weekend. My cousin eventually turned up in a taxi from Heathrow and my agent phoned the following Tuesday. No money was taken out of our bank account: our con-men hadn't been quick enough. We worked out that they probably made a point of pulling the scam late on a Friday when people would face a weekend without a land-line. Maybe they had insight and realised that lots of people have bill-reminders they've overlooked, or worry about not having paid properly. And it's a bonus for them if they find an older person, prone to panic and old enough not to have a mobile. Of course there was no way they could have known we had urgent incoming calls that day. That was purely a case of malign coincidence. Being the victim of any scam leaves you feeling very vulnerable. Still, the experience wasn't all bad – we did at least learn how to reconnect our land-line.

Jean, Stewart and Me

I was deeply upset to read a few weeks ago that Jean Simmons had died. I was once in love with her, as probably most good Englishmen now over retirement age were. And I had danced with her. It was at the Aida Foster School of Dance in Golders Green. I wasn't studying there myself, but a friend told me there were often dances on a Saturday night and there were never enough men to go round. I felt myself only just a man – those were modest, innocent times – but I enjoyed dancing, so I went along.

At some point during the evening, enjoying myself and slightly sweaty-palmed, I became aware of a truly beautiful girl dancing with someone else. I had to dance with her, but there would be a queue waiting. Then I looked and there wasn't. I wiped my palms on my handkerchief and seized the opportunity. It was a quickstep. We exchanged names. Jean Simmons had dark hair, sparkling brown eyes, and a very special voice. She told me she wanted to be an actress rather than a dancer. I was finding it hard to get words out but I told her I hoped to go to university. She was obviously older than I was, but as we grew older together what difference would a few years make? I didn't like to ask for her phone number during our first dance. I would ask later. There was no later. When I looked for her she was gone. The next time I saw her she was on a big screen playing a blonde Ophelia in Olivier's *Hamlet*.

I must admit that I wasn't as upset when she died as when I read, back in 1950, that she had married Stewart Granger. I never cared for him as an actor and so, as a man, how could he be worthy of Jean Simmons? To add insult to injury, shortly afterwards he decided on a Hollywood career and took his wife out there with him. Britain lost its best young actress and in the end Hollywood didn't really work out for either of them.

I was working in New York when I read that Jean Simmons had divorced Stewart Granger. It was 1960 and by then the few years' difference between us would have made no odds. A few months later, however, she married the American director Richard Brooks.

Seven years later I was back in London trying to be a serious writer. Fortunately I had a good agent and he found me other occasional work to make the hard times softer. Some of it consisted of being a script-doctor, rewriting other people's often disastrous screenplays. This way I met that rare bird in the film world, a nice, warm, intelligent director called Cyril Frankel. He was going to direct a fairly low-budget British thriller with a strong British cast, but he was having trouble with his star over the script. The star was Stewart Granger.

The Trygon Factor had an ingenious plot and some poor dialogue. Granger played a Scotland Yard inspector. The trouble was, as Frankel explained, the inspector has an affair with one of the younger women in the story. The producers felt that Scotland Yard inspectors didn't do that sort of thing. More discreetly, they were also concerned that Granger, then in his mid-fifties, was too old to carry this off. My job would be to shift the romance elsewhere and improve the dialogue. It didn't seem too hard a task for the money they were offering. I did it quickly and Frankel was pleased with my rewrite.

But the director wasn't out of the woods yet. There had been some harsh words between him and his star, who now wanted to talk to me – on my own. I didn't think that was a good idea. Frankel did. 'Remember, even if he's difficult, the producers and I are behind you.' I'd rather they'd been in front of me, but they were paying me, so, not without some curiosity to see Jean Simmons's ex, I went to the flat in Grosvenor Square where Granger was staying.

He opened the door. He was in a Noël Cowardy silk dressing-gown and cravat. He gave me a dazzling smile, took me into the living-room and offered me a drink. He was still a very good-looking man, fine profile, silvering hair, an ageing romantic hero who was still probably pretty handy with a rapier. I couldn't shake off that image. Maybe Jean Simmons couldn't either. Anyway, when the smiling was over, there was no fencing: he came straight to the point – my rewrites. If memory serves, and to paraphrase him slightly: 'In the first script I read I get to go to bed with the leading lady, in the next draft I only get to kiss her. Now, in your version, I don't even get to fucking touch her.'

The irony hit me – in real life Granger had got the girl,

but in this unreal one I had been brought in to make sure he
didn't. I couldn't tell him that, or bring up the age problem,
so I mumbled something about the exigencies of the plot.
I'm sure he knew the real reason. He gave me a bad idea for
the script, a sort of face-saving open ending. I said I would
talk to Frankel about it. I never saw Stewart Granger again.
The film was made and the Scotland Yard inspector didn't
sleep with or 'fucking touch' anybody.

I saw Jean Simmons once more – on stage in London.
She was starring in *A Little Night Music*, my favourite
Sondheim musical. She was charming and poignant as
Desirée Armfeldt, the fading star who returns to perform
in her hometown and meets an old admirer. Afterwards
I thought of going to the stage door to see her, but what
would I say? 'You probably don't remember me, but...'?
Send in the clowns.

1963 AND ALL THAT

All of us over forty-seven realise that Philip Larkin was using poetic licence when he wrote: 'Sexual intercourse began in 1963.' He was very specific about the timing too – 'Between the end of the Chatterley ban and the Beatles' first LP.'

I agree with Larkin about the year, but not the events. There were two more relevant happenings that year: the Profumo scandal and the Duchess of Argyll's divorce case. For the first time the Press were totally explicit and hugely excited about the details and varieties of SI. It was written and talked about, if not actually performed, more frequently and graphically than ever before. At respectable dinner-parties words and practices were mentioned that had to be explained to the less worldly. I didn't need explanations as I'd recently returned from living in the worldliest bit of the New World – New York. I'd also had a connection with a protagonist in the Duchess of Argyll divorce scandal.

That 'connection', for want of a better word, was the Duchess's step daughter, Lady Jeanne Campbell, daughter of the eleventh Duke and, more importantly, Lord

Beaverbrook's favourite granddaughter. I had met her at
Life where we were both reporters and, as the token English,
we'd become friendly. The story about 'Jeannie', according
to her American colleagues, was that she was working on
the clipping-desk when Beaverbrook turned up in New
York and had lunch with his fellow Press tycoon, Henry
Luce (*Time*, *Life*, *Sports Illustrated*, *Fortune*). Beaverbrook
told Luce that his granddaughter was working for him.
When Luce heard in what a humble capacity, he immediately called his personnel department and the next day
Jeannie became a reporter.

Jeannie was fun – tall, what used to be called buxom,
and not too obviously a lady. For me she was always more
jolly hockey-sticks than *femme fatale*, so you could have
knocked me over with a feather when she confided that
she had become Henry Luce's mistress. Jeannie was then
twenty-eight, Luce fifty-eight.

Luce had a reputation with his staff for being aloof and
puritanical – maybe something to do with being brought
up in China by missionary parents. Anyway Jeannie had
clearly broken through all that. She confided to my wife
that he had told her she was the only woman who could
make him giggle and make him come.

Jeannie obviously trusted my discretion because she told
me about the handbag trick. She kept a spare handbag in
a drawer and left it on her desk if she wanted to be away
from work for a while. If anyone in her open-plan office
answered her phone, they would say, 'She can't have gone
far, her handbag's on the desk.' On the occasion when she
confided this, she had in fact gone very far – to London

for three days to help her father, to whom she was devoted. The Duke was divorcing the Duchess, and Jeannie helped him break into her Mayfair house to get the vital evidence. She didn't tell me exactly what it was, but she was jubilant. The case took four years of legal wrangling to come to court and only then, back in London, did I read about what Jeannie and her Dad had stolen – several volumes of the Duchess's salacious diaries and the Polaroid photos of her activities, of which the best known was of her with nothing on except her trademark pearl necklace, performing what the Edinburgh judge called 'a disgusting sexual activity' on a headless man (of course he had a head, but it wasn't in the photo). The missing head was rumoured to be either Duncan Sandys's, or Douglas Fairbanks Jnr's. Many years later there was fairly conclusive proof it was the latter's. In concluding his 40,000-word summing-up, the judge said that the Duchess had ceased to be satisfied with normal SI and had committed multiple adultery 'to gratify a debased sexual appetite'. Decree granted, the Duke lit a celebration bonfire in Argyll, and Jeannie, back in New York, her affair with Henry Luce over, married Norman Mailer. The marriage, which lasted just over a year, produced one child and much domestic violence, leading to a divorce in that magical year, 1963.

For a while I maintained a Christmas-card relationship with Jeannie and then it lapsed. Meanwhile she had returned to journalism after marrying and divorcing a rich farmer in South Carolina. Then no news till I read her obituary in September 2007 in the *Daily Telegraph*. She had died in her Greenwich Village apartment in her last remaining treasure – Napoleon's campaign bed. It mentioned that she'd received a large advance for her memoirs but had blown it on a Greek villa without ever putting paper in her typewriter.

She did, however, make a stunning appearance in someone else's memoirs – those of James C. Humes, a speechwriter for Presidents Kennedy and Johnson. He wrote that she had, in a period of eighteen months starting in – yes again – 1963, slept with three presidents, Kennedy in Washington, Krushchev in Moscow and Castro in Havana. Get out the feather – knock me down.

Larkin was right about 1963. It was a vintage year.

JUMPING SHIP

At a party, some time ago, I was confronted by an attractive young woman who clearly felt she knew me well, but couldn't remember from where. I was having the same experience. The elusive penny dropped for her first. 'Got it,' she said, 'I just didn't recognise you with your clothes on.' That was the moment my wife joined us – which would make a better story if she had, but fortunately she wasn't there. The explanation was innocent. I knew this woman from the local swimming pool, where we were regulars. As it was a municipal pool we swam between 7 and 9 am on weekdays, before it was awash with local schoolchildren.

I have this quasi-recognition experience quite often, usually in the street, or in shops. I smile at someone I can't quite place and they smile back, equally puzzled. The problem is that we regulars are used to seeing much more of one another than just face and hands. Over the years we have watched each other waxing fat and waning thin, seen summer tans turn into winter pallor, shy tadpoles change into aggressive frogs, and swimsuit styles go from baggy to suggestive and back again. I have been swimming regularly, you might say obsessively, pretty much every day for forty years – about fifteen minutes a day. At a minute a 25-metre length, I've worked out that's the equivalent of swimming to New York. Even if my crawl improves, I doubt I'll be around long enough to complete the return trip.

Regulars are nothing if not regular – in everything they do. Show me a regular, a male one anyway, and I can tell you in what cubicle he changes, how long he swims for, what strokes he does, and in what order he takes off and puts on his clothes. Invariably in the next cubicle to me was a man whom I rightly guessed had to be an accountant. Every morning he swam twenty lengths, alternating back stroke and breast stroke, and dried his toes individually from left to right. One morning he looked very bothered and I expressed concern. 'I lost count this morning. I think I only did eighteen.' 'Do two extra tomorrow,' I suggested helpfully. A few moments later I saw him sneak back into the pool for the missing two. I may be obsessive, but that's surely OCS – obsessive compulsive swimming.

Inevitably among the regulars there were 'characters'. Jack, in his late sixties, was an ex-circus performer. Most mornings he went to the high diving-board, hurled himself off, did two backward somersaults and screamed blood-curdlingly before hitting the water. Then Jack began to lose it. The only time I ever saw the two obligatory lifeguards move quickly was when Jack emerged from the changing rooms having forgotten to put on his swimsuit. A few weeks later Jack reversed his car into another in the carpark. Shortly afterwards he did the same, this time forwards, and was never seen on the high board again.

As well as accountants and circus-performers, there were

– it being North London – a number of intellectuals and/
or artists, including one of my neighbours, the playwright
Arnold Wesker. He was in the habit of using the hair dryer,
one of those hooded ones where you put a coin in a meter.
The very thorough and theatrical way he dried his thick
head of hair annoyed me. As I passed him swishing his hair
about one morning, I said, 'You shouldn't dry your hair
that way, Arnold.'

'Why not?'

'Because it works off the pool water that's heated. Bags of
chlorine in it. Bad for the hair follicles.'

Clearly Arnold was as ignorant about science as I was and
quickly moved away from the hair dryer. Next time I saw
him he said, 'I spoke to a scientist. He said all that stuff you
told me about chlorine and follicles was rubbish.'

I tried to give a friendly smile: 'I didn't think you'd take
me seriously.'

Shortly afterwards Arnold moved to West Wales, near the
sea. If he swims there he probably has to dry his hair on a
towel.

In a municipal pool one rubs shoulders with all sorts, but
that eventually became the problem. There were just too
many shoulders. As swimming was touted as the healthiest
all-round exercise, the pool became more crowded and
hygiene suffered. Then one morning in the changing-room
I saw cockroaches, a platoon of them on the march.

But it wasn't the cockroaches that were the last straw
– it was pool rage. An increasing number of people were
banging into each other and shouting. One morning I
heard a man shouting furiously at another man, who

shouted back, but less furiously. A lifeguard restored peace. I finished my swim and went home. Next morning the lifeguard told me what had happened just after I'd left. The shoutee was having a shower when the serious shouter came in and started to abuse him again. The man told him to shut up. The serious shouter then went to his locker, took out a knife, came back and stabbed the other man to death. The killer then grabbed his clothes and ran. People saw him – he was dark-haired and in his twenties, but nobody knew or recognised him. The victim was a young American working temporarily in London, someone who only used the pool very occasionally.

The next few mornings the pool was not unnaturally under a pall, the regular swimmers in shock. We swam silently. It had to be the quietest public pool in the country. The more sensitive of us gave the showers a miss. The full story of the horrible event emerged gradually. The killer had run down the main road and thrown the bloodstained knife into a front garden, where the police found it. Shortly afterwards they received a phone call from the killer's parents. Their son had confessed to them what he'd done in his terrible fit of anger. He stood trial for murder at the Old Bailey in June 1990. Found guilty, he was sentenced to life imprisonment.

I swam on for a while, despite shock, crowding and cockroaches. Maybe it was out of some kind of municipal loyalty, like someone clinging to the NHS before deciding to pay up and go private. A large and efficient health club had recently opened nearby. I went to view it. It was immaculately clean, the staff friendly and the water in the pool sparkled with only a sprinkling of bodies in it. I paid up and joined. The high membership fee wouldn't protect me from a stray psychopath, but at least I'd be taking my chances in more congenial surroundings.

Soon I noticed other regulars from the municipal pool were joining. At first they looked slightly embarrassed at being caught out having gone up-market, but soon we all took on the air of battle-scarred veterans. We reminisce about the bad old days, though nobody mentions the murder. There is a camaraderie about us municipal alumni that is noticeably missing among the other men in the spacious, shiny changing rooms. We have come up the hard way.

JUMPING FOR HALSMAN

Audrey Hepburn was photographed by the world's leading photographers, and there are eighty-one delightful portraits of her currently on exhibition at the National Portrait Gallery. Two of them are by Philippe Halsman. One of them, taken in 1959, was his seventy-fifth cover for *Life* magazine. Having a picture on the front cover of *Life* was the ultimate accolade for a photographer. When the magazine stopped publication in 1972 – the ubiquity of television largely killed off photo-journalism – Halsman held the record with 101 covers.

I was there when Halsman took that picture of Audrey Hepburn. I was a (very young) *Life* reporter, lucky enough to be assigned to cover this photo essay. There always had to be text to go with the pictures. Hepburn was just as one would imagine her from her films, charming, slightly elfin and with the grace of a trained dancer. She had once danced in the chorus of a West End stage revue. In his long career, Halsman had taken portraits of most of the world's leading statesmen, scientists, artists, and actors. He was one of a number of Central European photographers, many of them Jewish, who had fled Europe at the start of World War II, and ended up working for *Life* in New York. En route there were risks and hardships.

Halsman's early life was more dramatic and tragic than most. Born and brought up in Riga, Latvia, his father a dentist, his mother a head-teacher, Philippe was a talented student, and went to study electrical engineering at Dresden University. In the summer of 1928, he went with his parents and sister on holiday in the Austrian Tyrol. The Halsmans were unaware that the particular resort they chose was the centre of the Heimwehr, a nationalist paramilitary organisation, associated with much local crime. One morning, father and son went off for a short climb. Philippe went a little ahead, and when he looked back his father had disappeared. He raced back and saw his father's body lying at the bottom of a ravine. By the time he climbed down, others had found him. He had been murdered and robbed.

The town council, pressured by the Heimwehr, insisted that Philippe be charged with his father's murder. There was only the weakest circumstantial evidence, and the main motive the prosecution came up with was Freud's Oedipus theory. Nonetheless, Halsman was found guilty and sentenced to ten years imprisonment. The case became known as the Austrian Dreyfus Case. There was international protest and a petition signed by thousands, including Einstein, Thomas Mann, and Freud, who protested about the misuse of his theory at the trial. Halsman served two years of his sentence before being pardoned by the President of Austria. After recovering from tuberculosis, contracted in prison, Halsman, with his mother and sister, went to live in Paris. There, he started his career as a photographer, and was just building a reputation when the Nazis arrived. His mother and sister left for America. Halsman, still with a Latvian passport, had trouble getting a visa, and eventually escaped via Marseilles. He arrived in New York with only a camera to his name.

Both in front of and behind the camera, Halsman was a witty and engaging man. He had the ability to make his sitters feel they were not just subjects, but part of the photographic process. At the end of the sessions with Audrey Hepburn, he asked her to jump. He explained that it was not for publication, only for his private collection. Shoes off, she obliged with a wonderfully uninhibited jump. Sadly, that picture is not in the exhibition at the National Portrait Gallery.

This ability to relax people in front of the camera meant that at the end of the session when Halsman asked them to jump, they jumped. Naturally, he didn't ask anyone who he thought was not physically up to it. But he couldn't resist asking Supreme Court Justice Learned Hand, who was eighty-nine. The Judge said, 'It might kill me – but it's not a bad way to go.' Then he did a fine jump – and survived. As for the few who refused, Halsman put that down to their fear of losing dignity – 'anyone who has real dignity cannot lose it in a jump.' Eventually he was persuaded to collate and publish his jumping photographs, and, in 1959, *Philippe Halsman's Jump Book* was published with a cast of 178 distinguished jumpers and the dedication 'To my subjects who defied gravity.' In the introduction, Halsman, tongue-in-cheek, expresses his new theory of Jumpology. 'The Prince de Talleyrand said that the tongue was given to diplomats to hide their thoughts... The face was given us to hide our inner selves. But one of our deepest urges is to find out what the other person is like... In a jump, with a sudden burst of energy, the subject cannot simultaneously control his expression, his facial or limb muscles. The Mask falls. One only has to snap it with a camera. Other psychological methods are lengthy and costly, the jump is rapid and economical.' In other words, don't go to an analyst or therapist, find a good photographer and jump.

Halsman claimed that jumping also showed national characteristics. The British were more reticent in their jumping than Americans. Churchill wasn't asked, Mountbatten, Bertrand Russell and Nye Bevan refused, Hugh Gaitskell soared very high, and the Duke and Duchess of Windsor jumped together holding hands, and then separately. Halsman was told that no self-respecting Frenchman would jump. He tried. The Prime Minister, Mendès-France and Jean Cocteau said 'non', Maurice Chevalier and Fernandel jumped, and the novelist Romain Gary jumped several times, then pleaded with Halsman for one more shot: 'I feel I have not expressed myself completely.'

Did Halsman himself ever deign to jump for the camera? Only once, and then it was in the company of Marilyn Monroe. His daughter Irene took the picture. After Audrey, I was to work twice more with him. I've always regretted that he never asked me to jump. I could have learned, early in life, so much about myself. At our last meeting, he gave me an inscribed copy of the *Jump Book*. It is a joyous book, and perfect for the coffee-table. Once opened, it stops people talking, and keeps them smiling for at least three-quarters of an hour.

MIXING WITH MANDRAKES

Writers have traditionally supplemented meagre incomes from their books by freelance journalism. As a very young novelist, I was trying to do just this in the early sixties and it wasn't easy. National newspapers, dailies and Sundays, as well as magazines, were closing down on Fleet Street and beyond. There were many explanations for this – rising production costs, restrictive union practices, bad labour relations, but, primarily, too many papers chasing too few readers and advertisers at a time when television was getting into every living-room. There was therefore some relief among the scribbling classes when a new quality Sunday paper started up in April 1961.

The *Sunday Telegraph*'s first editor was Donald McLachlan, a tall, austere-looking man in his late fifties. He had taught at Winchester and had a distinguished war record in Naval Intelligence before becoming a journalist. Something of the Wykehamist still clung to him and going to see him was like being sent for by the headmaster. I managed to get some features into the early issues of the paper that attracted McLachlan's attention. I was summoned to the

Beak's office and he suggested that I might like to join the staff. I was flattered but confused. Here finally was the offer of a good steady job on Fleet Street. I knew my parents, maybe even my wife, would bless the name of McLachlan and relax about my future. But I also knew that it was an offer I had to refuse. A full-time job would prevent me finishing my brilliant new novel. It was my wife who suggested some sort of compromise might be possible with McLachlan – something that was not full-time but less spasmodic than occasional pieces.

I carried her message, masquerading as my own, back to the editor. Too bad, he said. After a thoughtful pause he asked me if I knew Bobby Birch? I didn't know him, I said, but he had been editor of the now defunct *Picture Post* when I first went there as an unhappy management trainee. Well, he said, Bobby Birch was now Mandrake and he was desperate to find someone to help him. Mandrake was the *Sunday Telegraph*'s answer to the *Sunday Times*'s Atticus and the *Observer*'s Pendennis, both columns at the time having reputations for being well-informed, witty and well-written. McLachlan assured me that Birch and I would be equal partners. 'Decide between yourselves which of you is man and which drake.' McLachlan didn't make many jokes and he enjoyed that one. I was more amused by the idea of working alongside someone who had been at the top of the tree when I had been at the very bottom. I realised that wasn't a kind thought. It was more sad than amusing that someone who had edited a national magazine should now, no doubt in his fifties, end up as man or drake on a Sunday newspaper. When I met Bobby Birch I realised there were extenuating circumstances, more extraordinary than either sad or amusing.

Bobby Birch was indeed in his mid-fifties and looked every day of it. This was not too surprising as he was Britain's most married man. He was on wife number six when I met him and eventually outstripped Henry and made it to seven. I never had the courage to ask him outright why he chose to be a serial husband rather than a serial adulterer. One wasn't quite so frank about colleagues' private lives in those days. Bobby was still very handsome in a Rupert Brookeish way and extraordinarily charming. I was aware when I walked with him in the street that women of a certain age actually turned and looked at him. When it came to marriage I suspect he may have been the hunted rather than the hunter.

Bobby Birch welcomed me to the other half of his office and his job. It was agreed that I would do two-and-half days a week and so would he. He did indeed come into the office for that time, which was entirely different from working for that time, or even being there continuously for that time. I soon discovered that Bobby had another passion besides women – horses. He arrived with the first edition of the *Evening Standard* that gave all the races for the day and a summary of all the tipsters. He studied this carefully with a mug of coffee. That left about fifteen minutes to discuss what we ought to think about putting in the column for that week. Then he was off to Joe Coral down Fleet Street. Placing his bets took time as he bet on

every race at every meeting in Britain every day. And it
wasn't your common-or-garden 'to win' or 'each-way' bet.
It was a complicated network of doubles and trebles and
maybe even quadruples. The 2 o'clock at Uttoxeter was
cross-permed with the 3.30 at Lingfield Park, the 2.30 at
Newmarket with the 4 o'clock at Market Rasen. He would
return to the office for the early part of the afternoon to
see how I was getting on, do a little phone calling on one
of his own stories, and then it was off to Joe Coral's again
to check on his winnings or his losses. He didn't like to
be asked how he'd done. It must have seemed a little like
having to talk about his marriages. I could sometimes tell
by his expression or his mood how he had done, but it
wasn't all that easy. Gamblers, I discovered, have enormous
amour propre about their skills.

Naturally with this routine Bobby was a busy and preoccupied man, but win or lose, he always found time to be
charming to me. I responded by devotedly holding the fort,
which of course meant doing most of the column myself.
I wasn't going to complain because, when all was said and
done, I was finally on Fleet Street and writing. No, I wasn't
going to complain. Bobby Birch had read the situation very
shrewdly.

If, under his general charm and decency, Bobby Birch
had a fault, it was a mild paranoia that somebody might
do him down professionally. After a stormy career, he had
clearly found a safe harbour at the *Sunday Telegraph*. He
had various families, not to mention stables, to support
and didn't want anything to rock the boat. Obviously the

person he shared the column with had to be trustworthy and I assumed he thought I was. I had made it quite clear to him that I worked in order to find the wherewithal to be a novelist. I had no ambitions to be a managing editor or even a lone Mandrake. One week I realised he was a little edgy after McLachlan complimented us on two funny items in the column and they were both mine. I knew I would have to tread ultra-carefully. Our normal weekly routine was to dream up the various items on a Tuesday and some time on a Wednesday morning we both went into McLachlan's office to tell him what we had in mind. He would make his own suggestions or tell us if one of our ideas clashed with anything else planned for that Sunday.

One particular Wednesday McLachlan wanted to see us in a hurry and Bobby wasn't about. He may have been out Joe Coralling. I had no alternative but to go to the meeting alone and discuss our intended stories. I had an idea or two that I hadn't yet had time to discuss with Bobby. I sensed that he'd had a very bad week so far over the sticks at Uttoxeter and Market Rasen. One of my ideas was about what appeared to be our imminent entry into the Common Market. This particular mating dance had already been in progress for nearly a decade but now Macmillan seemed eager to reach some consummation. I had been at a party that weekend and the subject had come up, particularly concerning what adjustments the British male would have to make to be fully accepted on the continent. A rather drunk Portuguese had been very emphatic about our lack of skill in kissing. He wasn't talking, he said, about the

'French kiss' which we might by now be acquainted with, though distancing ourselves from it by attributing it to the French. He was talking about all the varied meanings and innuendoes in the kissing of female cheeks and hands of which we were totally ignorant. He gave me several examples. I suggested he could make a fortune if he gave private tuition, particularly in large companies with an eye to their export markets.

I told McLachlan about this. I planned to run the piece with illustrative photographs. I had a friend, a frequently 'resting' actor good at comic poses, who occasionally did this sort of thing for us. McLachlan seemed intrigued by how many ways the Portuguese could kiss the back of a woman's hand.

'Oh it's not just the back,' I said.

'Show me,' he said. He stood up, came round from behind his desk and held his hand out to me. My first reaction was that he was drunk. But it was 10.30 in the morning and he had a reputation for being extremely abstemious. He was known to be a little eccentric; now he had just gone over the edge and toppled into megalomania. Just my luck – I was merely the first hapless journalist who would be asked to kiss his hand that morning. It would be in all the other papers tomorrow. I took his hand.

'It's more romantic if you turn it over and kiss the palm,' I said, probably in a strangulated voice. I turned his hand over and quickly kissed the palm. As I straightened up I saw something horrific. McLachlan's office looked out over an internal well on the other side of which was the Mandrake office. One could only see the occupants of the opposite office if they were standing up and near the window. McLachlan and I were standing up near the window. Framed now in the other window was Bobby Birch, a look on his face I am unable even now, in such long retrospect, to describe.

'Are there more subtleties still?' McLachlan asked.

'He only told me one more,' I said.

'You'd better show me in case I go to Portugal,' McLachlan laughed. I'd never seen him within a hundred miles of being so jolly. Maybe the proprietor had doubled his salary and stock options that morning. I took his hand again.

'If you kiss the inside of the wrist it means...' I bowed over his wrist, turned it and kissed it beside his watch-strap. He finished the sentence for me, '... more serious intentions.'

'Yes,' I said, glancing over his shoulder at the window across the well. Bobby Birch was still there, frozen. I knew what he was thinking – not only was the editor of the *Sunday Telegraph*, despite his wife and three children, a raving homosexual, but he had forced Bobby to share his office and his job with another one. They were probably lovers. Now in some bizarre gay ritual of gratitude I was thanking McLachlan for getting rid of Bobby and appointing me as the one and only Mandrake.

'That should make a funny story,' McLachlan said.

That seemed to be the end of our meeting. I didn't wait for him to say 'Aren't you going to kiss me goodbye?' I scooped up my papers and left.

When I got back to the office Bobby was waiting. 'What the hell was that all about?'

'Going into the Common Market,' I said.

We took the photos and ran them the following week. McLachlan complimented us on them. Fortunately he liked one of Bobby's stories too. A few months later General de Gaulle said his famous 'Non' to our entry into the Common Market. Forty years later, after the kissing of millions of hands, the mating dance still goes on as we play hard-to-get over a new constitution and the old Euro.

In Bed with a Mammoth

I won't generalise and say 'all' or 'most', but certainly a great number of books these days, both fiction and non-fiction, are too long – hugely too long. Go into any bookshop, if you can find one, and look round. For some of the books on the higher shelves there should be a health and safety warning. If I could do my own illustrations I would draw, in the first box, an elderly woman reaching up for a book on the top shelf. In the second box, she is lying prostrate on the floor under the weight of Donna Tartt's *The Goldfinch,* all 864 pages of it. My wife, however, wanted to read it – till she saw it. She was particularly incensed by a quote on the cover, 'A book that's impossible to put down.' 'And impossible to pick up,' she said. Last year's Booker Prize winner, Eleanor Catton's *The Luminaries,* weighs in at 832 pages, Hilary Mantel's *Wolf Hall* at 559 pages, and her *Bringing Up the Bodies* at a modest 407.

Is there some deep cultural reason for this obesity? Do publishers really believe their readers really want these mammoth reads? A lot of writers lay the blame on editors who 'ain't what they used to be.' Some critics think that in building up best-selling novelists, publishers have created their own Frankenstein's monster. Sam Jordison, reviewing *The Goldfinch* in *The Guardian* writes, 'Editing Donna Tartt must be a daunting task. It would take an editor with steel *cojones* to ask her to trim down some of her 864 pages.' I suspect that if less successful writers were to send in anything over 300 or so pages they'd be told to do something very unhygienic with them.

One thing editors don't seem to have asked themselves is where can you comfortably read a book like that – certainly not in bed, even when it's in paperback. Unless you do regular press-ups in a gym, after half-a-dozen pages your arms ache, unless of course you buy one of those book-support things they slide over your bed in good hospitals. There is another more serious problem, if you've had a hard day. Doze off while you're reading and, by the law of gravity, there's only one place for the book to drop. Over 500 pages, especially in hardback, can cause bruising or tooth loss. Recently, and foolhardily, I took Neil MacGregor's brilliant *Germany: Memories of a Nation* (598 pages) to bed, and, frankly, I'm lucky not to have concussion.

Isn't this where Kindle comes in? Not in our house it doesn't. I can see the advantages of it while travelling, particularly on economy airlines, but not among the comforts of home and bed. Also if you put 500 or more pages into a Kindle and enlarge the print slightly, you get finger fatigue from sliding over the pages. Anyway, nowadays one spends so much time staring at screens, computers, mobiles and iPads, that there is something wonderfully reassuring about having a proper book in one's hands.

But, thanks to Peter Cooke and Dudley Moore, my wife and I have now solved our problem. I was in bed reading *One Leg Too Few*, William Cook's funny but tragic biography of the pair. It was genuinely hard to put down, but I had to. At 566 pages, it is heavy even in paperback. I moaned to my wife, 'Why can't they publish books like this in two volumes?' I fell asleep before I heard her answer. Next morning, I was having breakfast, my book propped up on the marmalade jar, when my wife arrived brandishing a Stanley knife. 'I've got the solution,' she said. I didn't catch on. 'To our marriage?' 'No, to those books.' She took my book, closed it, and opened it exactly in the middle of the binding. 'After all it's only a paperback,' she said and, ever practical, sliced it carefully down the middle. I now had Pete and Dud in two volumes – and very comfortable reading they were too.

Maybe this is sacrilege to a true book-lover, but to a practical reader it is a great blessing. After all, one couldn't do it to a hardcover, or a library book, and what were paperbacks first designed for – to fit neatly in your pocket or read easily in bed. Shortly after this, my wife came back from the bookstore with two novels she had always meant to read. She took them out of the bag and the Stanley knife out of the drawer. She now has four volumes of Hilary Mantel to look forward to.

ONE WEDDING AND NO SPEECHES

When I first met him the late and great Bernard Levin was the drama critic of the *Daily Mail*, and he and the *Evening Standard* critic, Milton Shulman, were known as the kosher butchers. I was fortunate that by the time I had a play on in town Bernard had given up drama criticism and moved onto higher things – a column in *The Times* and a regular slot on *That Was the Week that Was*. In fact, he was already quite a star when he agreed to 'appear' in my first play. He told me his only other stage appearance had been as one of the old ladies in a school production of *Arsenic and Old Lace*.

Though he had some good lines, it was a small part, but maybe Bernard was intrigued by the originality of the idea. Previously when one wanted to show someone watching television on stage it was only the back of the television set that faced the audience. The actor faced the screen and a sound tape of what he or she was watching was used. I had a good reason for not wanting it that way. My leading lady was a sociologist who had written a learned book concerned with sex, and, inevitably, she was being turned into a TV pundit while her own sex life was going to the dogs. (Well, it was a first play.) I wanted the audience actually to see the reactions of the character while she was watching herself on television. In order to do this we pre-filmed her being interviewed by Bernard and thus were able to play this with the screen visible to the audience. It worked a treat but the play still closed after six weeks. Bernard remained a friend and thereafter always referred to the experience as 'our play'.

When Bernard joined *The Times* it advertised him as 'savage, cunning, witty and brilliant,' and I had always been somewhat in awe of him. My own day-job at the time was as an editor on *Town,* a smart, glossy magazine that didn't outlive the Swinging Sixties. I mightn't have been that 'witty and brilliant', but I did have the advantage of a beautiful secretary with whom Bernard was in love. I saw, or rather heard, the progress of his very romantic but bumpy courtship at fairly close quarters – an unavoidable eavesdropper on telephone conversations in a small, shared office. The problem was that Bernard's inamorata was torn between him and a reporter on *The Sunday Times*. The latter eventually won out. Bernard was invited to the wedding, and so were my wife and I.

The wedding was a very grand affair in a smart Kensington church with the reception in a nearby hotel. The men were all in morning suits and the women in very fancy hats and summer dresses. The reception was only getting into its swing when Bernard came up to me and said *sotto voce* (he was a great opera-lover), 'I can't take any more of this. Let's go to the races – Sandown Park. I'm invited to the Variety Club Meeting there. We're dressed for Tattersall's.

I've a car outside.' I put it to my wife, who felt as sorry for the love-lorn Bernard as I did. So the three of us discreetly scarpered.

As Bernard didn't drive, the car parked round the corner was a rented Daimler. Bernard gave instructions to the dark-suited driver to proceed to Sandown Park. He had two tickets and insisted on paying for the third. It was a beautiful afternoon. We inspected the horses and the other celebrities, though Bernard, now very recognisable from television, hated people staring at him. Luck ran our way, at least for the first couple of races, and Bernard cheered up. We'd just collected our second lot of winnings at the Tote, when I saw a lady in a bright red dress pointing Bernard out to a girl of about fourteen. She handed her race card to the girl, clearly her daughter, and pushed her towards Bernard. The girl came up, awkwardly offered him the card and a pen, and asked for his autograph.

'Oh, you don't want mine. You want his.' He smiled and pointed at me. 'He's the famous one.'

Even more awkwardly, the girl passed me the card and pen. I felt I had no option but to write 'With best wishes' and sign my name. As she went I said to Bernard, not so *sotto voce*, 'Bastard.' I watched her go back to her mother and show the card. I didn't need to be a lip-reader to know what she was saying – 'Who the hell's Stanley Price?' The girl looked aggrieved. I couldn't make out what she said to her mother, but I hope it was: 'If Bernard Levin says he's famous he must be famous.' Anyway I lost on the next three races and was pleased Bernard did too.

I didn't see a lot of Bernard over the next few years and

then heard he hadn't been well. There was a rumour of Alzheimer's. We exchanged notes. Some time later I was walking in Regent's Park and saw Bernard coming towards me. I knew he had a flat nearby. He was accompanied by a much younger woman who gently held his arm. He looked at me without any recognition and I saw the vague look in his eye. I couldn't face having to explain who I was, or how he knew me. I let him go by. I didn't want to remember him that way. I'd rather think of the Andy Warhol remark about 'famous for fifteen minutes' and remember how Bernard had made me famous for about three. Because of him I'd lost money, missed the speeches, and had one of the best afternoons I've ever had.

WHERE WERE YOU FOR CHURCHILL'S FUNERAL?

B efore he presented the documentary on the fiftieth anni-versary of Winston Churchill's funeral, Jeremy Paxman said: 'I was only a schoolboy at the time, but the funeral made a huge impression on me'. It had the same effect on me, although I was no longer a schoolboy. Presumably like Paxman, I saw it on television, but probably under slightly more unusual circumstances.

I was in London trying to finish a book (writing, not reading) when an American magazine for which I occasion-ally wrote asked me if I would go to Ireland to interview Richard Burton. He was currently filming *The Spy Who Came in from the Cold* at the Ardmore Studios at Bray, just outside Dublin. I felt I could spare a few days from my literary career to talk to Richard Burton. It would also be a good way to clear my conscience and visit two elderly aunts who lived together in Dublin.

I contacted the publicity officer at the studio and made an appointment to see Burton. I was warned that he had a tight schedule and I might have to hang around a little. A couple of days later I presented myself at the Ardmore Studios and hung round more than a little. Finally, however, I was taken to Burton's dressing-room, and introduced to the world's most famous couple. Elizabeth Taylor was visiting her husband. This was during their first marriage, and he had not yet given her the world's second-largest diamond. Her violet eyes were indeed strikingly beautiful, but she was well known for putting on weight between jobs, and she was between jobs. Her hair was a bit wild too, so I didn't fall disastrously in love with her. Burton, however, looked in good shape. His face was a bit harrowed, but that was make-up for his next scene where he was being interrogated by the Stasi. They were both charming and friendly, if a little distracted.

My attempts to interview Burton were constantly inter-rupted by the telephone. They each had a private line and were often both talking at the same time. Between calls they were apologetic. From what I heard, I gathered that Liz was having trouble getting a vet to visit her dogs, in private quarantine on their yacht parked somewhere in the Thames estuary. There were also problems about the refurbishments to their house in LA. Burton was talking to a lawyer about Gaston, their chauffeur, who had apparently knocked somebody down in Dublin. It was, of course, a pleasure to listen to Burton's sonorous voice with its soft Welsh underlay, even if he wasn't talking to me. I felt flat-tered that, on such brief acquaintance, they were letting me share in their complex domestic lives, and learn that being rich and famous was not without its silly little worries.

Burton was now called to the set, and I went with him to watch the shooting. With the numerous takes for each scene, to cover the endless things that go wrong, it was soon clear that there wouldn't be a chance to talk to Burton again that day. The apologetic publicity man arranged for me to come back the following day. I dutifully returned to Ardmore the next morning, and was eventually shown into Burton's dressing-room. They were both there again, this time sitting in front of a large television set with an open bottle of champagne in an ice-bucket between them. Burton told me to pull up a chair and poured me a glass of champagne. He gestured at the screen: 'Just giving the old man a send-off.' In my trips to and from Ardmore, I had forgotten it was Saturday, 30th January. They were watching Churchill's state funeral.

On the screen the coffin, on a Union-Jack-draped gun-carriage, was being driven slowly from St Paul's through the city to the pier at the Tower of London. There was solemn music and the equally solemn sound of Richard Dimbleby's commentary. Burton was wearing a rather smart shirt and held out his arms to show me his big silver cufflinks. Burton nodded at the screen: 'Winston gave them to me.' Liz said that Richard had done his voice several times. He had done the narration for the four episodes of *The Valiant Years* on television: 'Did you see it?' With Churchill's coffin being transferred to a launch at Tower Pier with an umpteen gun salute in the background, I felt ashamed to admit that I had missed it. (Four years later I did see him playing Church-ill very convincingly in a television film of *The Gathering Storm*.)

Burton opened another bottle of champagne and topped up our glasses. I asked him how he had first met Churchill.

'He came to my dressing-room after *Hamlet* at the Old Vic. He said: 'My lord Hamlet, may I use your lavatory?' Burton leaned forward and turned off Dimbleby's commentary. With the launch going up-river from the Tower towards the Houses of Parliament, Burton now did his own commentary in Churchill's voice and with Churchill's own words. He had tears running down his cheeks. I looked over at Liz. She was crying too. I found myself joining in. At the Festival Hall pier, the coffin was transferred to an open carriage and driven to Waterloo, from where it was to go by train to the family plot at Bladon churchyard. Clutching champagne glasses, crying with the Burtons, watching Churchill on his last journey, was one of life's stranger experiences.

Afterwards, lunch was brought to the dressing-room. Our conversation got onto great performances – not in the theatre, but at Cardiff Arms Park and Lansdowne Road. Burton was a passionate rugby fan and Wales supporter. Liz clearly wasn't. She put an end to the conversation by offering me a lift back into Dublin. Naturally, I accepted. I sat in the back of the car with Liz, and Gaston drove. He was a large, dark Corsican in a black leather jacket. He drove very fast and, after what I'd heard, I was nervous. Fortunately, Liz took my mind off it. She had clearly had her hair done, was wearing a very agreeable perfume, and looked great. Maybe she had dressed up for Winston's funeral. I have to admit to the thought – if only my friends or relatives could see me now, sitting in the back of a black Bentley with Elizabeth Taylor. The only people likely to see us in Dublin, however, were my two elderly aunts, who hadn't got a television, rarely went to 'the pictures', and wouldn't know who the 'divil' she was. And, in those early days of celebrity culture, I couldn't even take a selfie.

MEETING THE MASTER

If one is going to name-drop there's no point in being half-hearted about it. I first met Noël Coward in Havana. It was in June 1959, just after Fidel Castro and his rebels, the *barbudos* (bearded ones) had taken over the capital, after three years of fighting their way through the mountains. General Fulgencio Batista had fled, in traditional dictatorial fashion, with his pockets stuffed with the public's pesos. I was a junior reporter on *Life* magazine and had just flown in from New York with Peter Stackpole, the photographer. The revolution was over and we were here to cover a safer form of shooting – the filming of Graham Greene's *Our Man in Havana*. Columbia Pictures had originally done a deal with Batista, but Castro said he would honour the contract and guarantee everybody's safety, an ambitious promise, given that the streets were still full of young men brandishing their sub-machine guns. Most of them looked almost too young to have grown the straggly beards that were their badge of honour.

So, within a few days of Castro coming to power, a second invasion arrived – Noël Coward, Alec Guinness, Maureen O'Hara, Ernie Kovacs, the director Carol Reed

and Graham Greene himself, who had written the screenplay. Peter Stackpole and I seemed to be the only journalists
yet to have arrived. We had this starry cast to ourselves.
We were all housed in a very luxurious hotel which revo-
lutionary socialist principles had not yet penetrated. The
décor was definitely Florida *mafiosi*. There was a flourishing
casino and two exotic bars, where, at tables round the wall,
appropriately exotic call-girls were waiting to provide room
service.

Our first night there, Peter Stackpole and I went out for
a late Latin dinner. In the main square there were umpteen
thousand people, all staring upwards at a balcony, where
Fidel himself was haranguing them, *cincuenta* to the dozen.
Retracing our steps after dinner, at least two hours later,
there were still umpteen thousand people in the square –
perhaps not the same umpteen – but all staring up at Fidel
still in full flow on the balcony.

Inevitably, when shooting started, a vast crowd of
Havanistas were out on location to see the action, but
the *barbudos* kept them at firearms-length from the film
crew and actors. I watched Noël Coward's first scene. He
appeared, walking down a crowded Havana street, wearing
a dark city suit, collar, tie and homburg. Later, at a nearby
café, with an armed guard in attendance who Coward kept
shooing away, he told me it was his 'English spy abroad
outfit'. He was playing Hawthorne, an MI6 agent investi-
gating one of his local agents, Wormald (Alec Guinness), a
vacuum-cleaner salesman, who had been sending sketches
of mysterious missile sites in the countryside. It turned
out that they were scaled-up sketches of vacuum-cleaner

parts. Greene's black comedy of Cold War espionage clearly appealed to Coward, as both men had had dealings with MI6 during the war. At the time of filming, none of us knew how prophetic Greene's story was. Three years later, in October 1962, Kennedy faced down Krushchev in the Cuban missile crisis – except it wasn't vacuum-cleaning parts the Russian convoy was intent on delivering.

Havana's most famous resident at this time was Ernest Hemingway. He had settled there after World War II, and wrote the novels that were to win him both the Nobel and Pulitzer Prizes. Apparently, when he came into town, he always drank at Sloppy Joe's bar. The unit publicist tipped me off that Hemingway would be there next day for a meeting with his old friend, Noël Coward. We would have to be very discreet about taking a picture as Sloppy Joe was very protective of 'Poppa' Hemingway. I realised that it would be a great *coup* to get a discreet picture of Hemingway and Coward with Graham Greene. Next morning, I looked everywhere for Greene, but he had disappeared. Peter had to settle for just two of the world's most famous writers. They seemed to be enjoying each other's company, but there was no way to eavesdrop discreetly. Anyway, I had all the material I wanted, Peter had enough pictures, other journalists had begun to show up in town. It was time to head back to New York.

Six years later, I was at a first night in the West End – my own. It was my first play and afterwards in a crowded dressing-room I came face-to-face with Noël Coward. The play's producer, Binkie Beaumont, a great friend of Coward's, introduced us.

'We've met before, haven't we?' Coward said, 'but where?'
'Havana.'

'Of course – all those young men waving guns about.' He said it was the nearest he'd ever come to being properly shot in a film. We reminisced briefly about the film and he said some nice things about my play. As he was leaving, Binkie asked where he was heading next.

'Bury St Edmunds. George Baker's just restored that old Georgian theatre there. They're opening it tomorrow with *Private Lives*.' He paused. 'I go to Bury St Edmunds – not to praise him.'

There was no capping a Coward exit line. He was not called 'the Master' for nothing. For me, it was a definitive exit line. I never met him again. He died six years later, in 1973, aged seventy-three.

Ten years later, I went to a memorial service in Westminster Abbey where a plaque was unveiled to him in the South Choir Aisle. The Queen Mother laid her wreath, followed by the knights and dames of the acting profession. In the background, Coward's music played – 'London Pride', 'Mad Dogs and Englishmen' and, most poignantly, 'I'll Follow My Secret Heart.' Then the Queen Mother led the procession out of the Abbey with Graham Payne, Coward's long-time partner, at her side. The Master would have appreciated that.

STANLEY PRICE

Stanley Price was born in London of Irish parents on 12th August 1931. His grandparents were Lithuanian Jews who had emigrated to Ireland. He went to schools in Dublin and London, where his father had come to work as a GP. After National Service he went up to Gonville and Caius College, Cambridge, where he read History. After graduating he spent a brief period in magazine publishing in London. In 1956 he emigrated to America and spent four years working as a reporter on *Life* magazine. He worked mainly in the Entertainment Department, writing about films and theatre. In 1962 he returned to London and his first novel, *Crusading for Kronk*, was published in 1961. This was quickly followed by *The Biggest Picture* (1962), *Just for the Record* (1963) and *A World of Difference* (1965). All four were published in the US and the UK, and the last two in paperback by Penguin.

In 1967 his first West End play, *Horizontal Hold*, was produced by the celebrated Binkie Beaumont of HM Tennant, but had the misfortune to open on the same night as the Six-Day War. He had two subsequent West End successes: *Moving* (1982), with Penelope Keith, about the trauma of moving house, and *Why Me?* (1985), with Richard Briers, about the problems of executive unemployment. *Why Me?*, John Peter wrote in *The Sunday Times*, created a new genre, 'something half-way between a realistic farce and a situation tragedy – a sitrag, as opposed to a sitcom.' A more outright farce, *The Starving Rich* (1972), set in a health clinic, had two UK tours, never came into London, but has since been produced internationally in France, Spain, Holland, and especially Germany.

In the late 1960s and early 1970s, when the British film industry, backed by American investment, was booming, Stanley wrote, but mostly rewrote, screenplays, including *Arabesque* (1965), with Gregory Peck and Sophia Loren, *Gold* (1974), with Roger Moore and Susannah York, and *Shout at the Devil* (1977), with Lee Marvin and Roger Moore. His original screenplays were written for television. *Close Relations* and *Genghis Cohn*, both for BBC2, respectively won the Reims International Television Festival's best screenplay award in 1990, and its Jury Prize for best film in 1995. *Genghis Cohn* also won the 1995 US Cable TV Ace Award for best screenplay. Between 1981 and 1985 Stanley also dramatised four Noël Coward short stories for the BBC, including *The Kindness of Mrs Radcliffe* and *Star Quality*, and in 1997 wrote a drama-documentary, *A Royal Scandal*, about the Queen Caroline Affair.

In his last years Stanley turned to non-fiction. In 2003 he published a memoir, *Somewhere to Hang my Hat: An Irish-Jewish Journey*, and in 2012, with his son Munro Price, *The Road to Apocalypse: The Extraordinary Journey of Lewis Way*. Both were shortlisted for the *Jewish Quarterly* –

Wingate Literary Prize. His last book, *James Joyce and Italo Svevo: The Story of a Friendship*, described by Jan Morris in the *Literary Review* as 'admirable ... so rich in detail and characterization', appeared in 2016. He also, of course, became a regular contributor to *The Oldie*.

Stanley died on 28th February 2019.

ACKNOWLEDGEMENTS

THE COLLATOR would like to thank *The Oldie* for giving permission to reprint Stanley's pieces, Maureen Lipman for her foreword, and Sam Carter for bringing everything together in such a handsome volume.